Reducing Business Jet Carbon Footprint

Reducing
Business Jet
CARBON
FOOTPRINT

Using the Power of the
Aircraft Electric Taxi System
A Multi Case Study

DR. THOMAS F. JOHNSON

NEW YORK

LONDON • NASHVILLE • MELBOURNE • VANCOUVER

Reducing Business Jet CARBON FOOTPRINT

Using the Power of the Aircraft Electric Taxi System, A Multi Case Study

© 2023 Dr. Thomas F. Johnson

Published in New York, New York, by Morgan James Publishing. Morgan James is a trademark of Morgan James, LLC. www.MorganJamesPublishing.com

Proudly distributed by Ingram Publisher Services.

Morgan James BOGO™

A **FREE** ebook edition is available for you or a friend with the purchase of this print book.

CLEARLY SIGN YOUR NAME ABOVE

Instructions to claim your free ebook edition:
1. Visit MorganJamesBOGO.com
2. Sign your name CLEARLY in the space above
3. Complete the form and submit a photo of this entire page
4. You or your friend can download the ebook to your preferred device

ISBN 9781636980973 case laminate
ISBN 9781636980980 eBook
Library of Congress Control Number: 2022948849

Cover Design by:
Christopher Kirk
www.GFSstudio.com

Interior Design by:
Chris Treccani
www.3dogcreative.net

Morgan James is a proud partner of Habitat for Humanity Peninsula and Greater Williamsburg. Partners in building since 2006.

Get involved today! Visit: www.morgan-james-publishing.com/giving-back

Dedicated
in loving memory to
my mother,
Helen Alberta Goodell

TABLE OF CONTENTS

Introduction   *xv*

Preface   *xvii*

Chapter 1: Introduction   1

Chapter 2: Business Jets and Their Carbon Footprints   3

Chapter 3: Benefits of the Business Jet Electric Taxi System 57

Business Jet Braking System Enhancement   59

Fuel Consumption Evaluation During Ground Taxi   61

Emissions Reduction During Ground Taxi   62

Airport Area Air Pollution   69

European Environmental Research Input   72

Middle Eastern Environmental Research Input   73

Increased Aircraft Usage Between Engine Overhauls   79

Airport Ground Safety   80

Airport Area Noise Reduction   85

Foreign Object Damage "FOD" Reduction   86

Operational Cost Reduction   87

Chapter 4: Business Jet Aircraft Landing Gear   **89**

    Nosewheel Drive Installations   90

    Main Gear Drive Installations   90

    Advantages of the Tandem Gear Box

    Nosewheel Steering   92

Chapter 5: The Future of the Business Jet Electric Taxi System 95

Appendix A   98

Appendix B   99

Appendix C   100

Appendix D   101

Appendix E   102

Appendix F   103

Appendix G   104

Appendix H   105

Appendix I   106

Appendix J   107

Appendix K   108

Appendix L   109

Appendix M   110

Appendix N   111

Appendix O   112

Appendix P   113

Appendix Q   114

Appendix R   115

Appendix S   116

Appendix T   117

Appendix U   118

Appendix V   119

Appendix W   120

Appendix X   121

Appendix Y   122

Appendix Z   123

Appendix AA   124

Appendix BB   125

Appendix CC   126

Appendix DD   127

Appendix EE   128

Appendix FF   129

Acknowledgments   *131*

About the Author   *133*

LIST OF FIGURES

Figure 1 Cessna Citation X   xix

Figure 2 Decibel Scale   84

Figure 3 Honeywell HTF7500 Gas Turbine Engine
Inlet Guide Vanes   85

Figure 4 Gulfstream G650   88

Figure 5 Tandem Gear Drive with Motors Installed   91

Figure 6 Electric Taxi System Tandem Gear Box Nosewheel   92

Figure 7 Typical Business Jet Main Landing Gear Wheel
with Electric Motors   93

Figure 8 Embraer Legacy 650   94

LIST OF TABLES

Table 1 PW 1500G Emissions Data   76

Table 2 Honeywell HTF7000 Emissions Data   78

INTRODUCTION

The business jet "carbon footprint" is defined as the total greenhouse gas emissions emitted by the aircraft main propulsion gas turbine engines. This is expressed as carbon dioxide equivalent. Greenhouse gases are emitted through the business jet engine exhaust. The aircraft engine manufacturers are required to measure and publish the amount of quantifiable greenhouse gases their engines produce. The description, performance, and the carbon footprint left behind, as published by the International Civil Aircraft Organization (ICAO), are discussed with the focus on forty-five of the day's most popular medium- to large-sized business jets.

Some countries/governments are charging a "carbon tax," to be paid by the operator of the aircraft when the aircraft is operated within their borders. The policymakers define the monetary fee on each ton of carbon and tax the aircraft owner accordingly. The carbon tax money, when collected, is distributed to fund renewable energy projects like wind power, solar farms, etc. When a country, company, airline, or other entity claims to be carbon neutral, this means they have calculated the amount of greenhouse gases they produce and have invested in renewable energy to offset the air pollution they generate.

—uptake of CO2 via biological processes Greenhouse gases emitted + release of CO2 via biological processes Solar farms, wind generators, trees + replacing polluted air = 0
Boston University; Boston, MA (https://sites.bu.edu)

The amount of greenhouse gas emitted by each business jet aircraft during all normal ground and flight operations is published along with other aircraft engine certification data for the specific make and model of aircraft. If the country the aircraft is flying through has a carbon tax, the operator of the aircraft will get a carbon tax bill. When the business jet aircraft is certified for flight, either on the assembly line at the factory or recertified with the aftermarket electric taxi system, the published greenhouse gas emissions report will follow the aircraft through the aircraft registration number. If the aircraft is equipped with the electric taxi system, the emissions report will be smaller. As the carbon footprint of the business jet is reduced, the operator will pay less carbon taxes.

PREFACE

My previous book, published January 2021, *Reducing Airlines' Carbon Footprint: Using the Power of the Electric Taxi System*, is focused on the many benefits related to the use of electric power in commercial airliner aircraft taxiing operations. The improvement of airport air quality, the costs of the electric taxi system installation, and fuel consumption evaluations are calculated using theory, modeling, and simulation, since no operator has put the electric taxi system into service. These are both before and after electric taxi system installation, as related to the commercial airline industry.

These issues are discussed and important to both the airline and the business jet industry. Ground taxi time and improved airport terminal accessibility are also discussed in my last book and are important money-saving topics for the airlines, but not so much for the business jet community.

This book focuses on the business jet reduced fuel consumption, emissions reduction during ground taxi, increased aircraft usage between engine overhauls, ground safety, noise reduction, and foreign object damage (FOD) reduction. Damage is caused to the aircraft main engines by sucking up debris on the tarmac, and the aircraft suffers ground damage from the jet blast when it is taxiing while using the main engines.

This book details how the business jets that are equipped with the aircraft electric taxi system will be able to land, turn off the main engines, and taxi on the tarmac using electric power. The same is true for when it is time to leave on a trip. Load up your passengers, taxi to the runway run up area using the electric taxi system, and then start the engines for the first time. The actual cost of fuel savings and emissions reduction realized using the electric taxi system are discussed in detail for medium- to long-range business jets.

CESSNA CITATION X

CHAPTER 1:

Introduction

The business jet industry has grown tenfold over the past decade. The smaller aircraft jet engine manufacturers have come a long way to increase efficiency and reduce engine weight and fuel consumption. However, they are still emitting the same five bad constituents of gas turbine engine (GTE) exhaust emissions. Aircraft engine emissions are composed of carbon dioxide (CO_2), nitrogen dioxide/nitric oxide (NOx), carbon monoxide (CO), sulfur oxides (SOx), and volatile organic compounds (VOC), and others, aka the "carbon footprint."

The jet engine manufacturers have Federally mandated emissions target requirements to meet while the aircraft is at climb, cruise, and approach to landing thrust settings; however, there are no emissions targets while the engine is at idle or less than 10 percent thrust while taxiing on the ground. During taxi operations is when the gas turbine

1

engines are the least efficient and produce the emissions that do the most damage to the local airport environment. The business jets that are equipped with the aircraft electric taxi system (ETS) will be able to land, turn off the main engines, and taxi on the tarmac using electric power.

All aircraft engines have a manufacturer's recommendation for the operating time between engine overhauls (TBO). For the smaller business jet engines, like the Pratt & Whitney PT6 turbo prop, the TBO is 3,500 hours. For the larger engines, like the Honeywell family of HTF7000 engines, the TBO is 10,000 hours. The business jet with the electric taxi system installed will not be running the engines while the aircraft is on the ground during taxi and will not be adding engine operating hours to the end of the engine TBO period, therefore increasing the total aircraft usage time when the main engines are turned off, and the aircraft is taxiing using electric power.

CHAPTER 2:

Business Jets and Their Carbon Footprints

The electric taxi system kits could be retrofitted for aircraft currently in service or installed at the factory during production. The target-sized aircraft for the aircraft electric taxi system application should be the midsized to large business jets. Forty-five of the most popular makes and models are described in this chapter.

Cessna Citation III

Anyone familiar with the private jet industry knows about Cessna's line of Citation business jets: economic, high-performing, comfortable private jets that consistently stand out in the market. The Citation III is one private jet that strikes the perfect balance between cost, performance, and comfort. It can fly from the Midwest to either coast or nonstop from New York to Miami or Dallas.

The engines are the Pratt & Whitney Canada JT15D. This is a small turbofan engine built by Pratt & Whitney Canada. It was introduced in 1971 at 2,200 lbf (9,800 N) thrust and has since undergone a series of upgrades to just over 3,000 lbf (13 kN) thrust in the latest versions. It is the primary power plant for a wide variety of smaller jet aircraft, notably business jets (www.jetadvisors.com).

When the JT15D engine is operated during taxi at a 7 percent thrust, a typical twenty-six-minute ground taxi will generate 50.50 g/kg hydrocarbons, 132.00 g/kg of CO_2, and 1.7 g/kg of nitrogen oxides (times two engines). This is also known as the carbon footprint. This will be eliminated when the aircraft is using electrical power for ground taxi operations (see **Appendix A**).

Cessna Citation VI

Cessna's line of business jets, the Citations, is known for economy, reliability, and performance. They have consistently stood out in the market since the first Citation rolled off the line in 1972. Their major breakthrough into the private jet market came with the success of the Citation III, which won the Collier Trophy and cemented Cessna's reputation as a serious contender in the private jet market. The Citation VI is one of the updates for the Citation III; it is more economical both in acquisition cost and hourly operating cost (www.jetadvisors.com).

The Cessna Citation V1 is powered by two Honeywell TFE731-2-2B engines. When the TFE731-2-2B engine is operated during taxi at a 7 percent thrust, a typical twenty-six-minute ground taxi will generate 20.04 g/kg hydrocarbons, 58.60 g/kg of CO_2, and 2.82 g/kg of nitrogen oxides (times two engines). This is also known as the carbon footprint. This will be eliminated when the aircraft is using electrical power for ground taxi operations (see **Appendix B**).

Cessna Citation Vll

The Citation VII is the high-end version of the Citation VI. It uses different engines to increase cruise speed and takeoff performance. The cabin is more comfortable, featuring improved design options and increased soundproofing. The most distinctive difference between the Citation VII and the Citation VI is its upgraded engines. It comes equipped with two Honeywell TFE731-3 engines, flat rated to 4,080 pounds of thrust each—780 pounds more than the engines used on the Citation VI. These engines improve takeoff performance by 180 feet at sea level and by 630 feet at high-altitude airports. Its climb rate is improved as well—it can reach 37,000 feet in eighteen minutes. It cruises between 417 and 459 knots and is a good choice for short trips (www.jetadvisors.com).

When the TFE731-3 engine is operated during taxi at 7 percent thrust, a typical twenty-six-minute ground taxi will generate 9.04 g/kg hydrocarbons, 47.70 g/kg of CO_2, and 3.72 g/kg of nitrogen oxides (times two engines).

This is also known as the carbon footprint. This will be eliminated when the aircraft is using electrical power for ground taxi operations (see **Appendix C**).

Gulfstream G150

Announced in September 2002, Gulfstream partnered with Israel Aircraft Industries to introduce the Gulfstream G150. It would replace the G100 in production in 2006. This medium-range, multiengine turbofan business aircraft lives up to Gulfstream's standards of reliability and high performance in private jets. The G150 is powered by two fuel-efficient Honeywell TFE731-40AR-200G turbofan engines. Each engine produces 4,420 pounds of thrust, both supplied with full authority digital engine control (FADEC). Their inspection interval is 6,000 hours (www.jetadvisors.com).

When the TFE731-40AR-200G engine is operated during taxi at a 7 percent thrust, a typical twenty-six-minute ground taxi will generate 9.00 g/kg hydrocarbons, 45.70 g/kg of CO_2, and 3.1 g/kg of nitrogen oxides (times two engines). This is also known as the carbon footprint. This will be eliminated when the aircraft is using electrical power for ground taxi operations (see **Appendix D**).

Hawker Beechcraft Hawker 750

Originating from the 1962 de Havilland DH.125 medium-sized corporate jet, the Hawker 750 is a light-to-midsize jet based on the 800 model. The Hawker 750 has more baggage space and a larger cabin than its predecessor, even claimed as the largest cabin in the class by Hawker. Like the entire Hawker family, the aircraft upholds the company's high reliability and performance standards. Deliveries of the Hawker 750 began in 2008.

The Hawker 750 is powered by two Honeywell TFE-731-5B engines rated at 4,660 pounds of thrust apiece and with an inspection interval of 4,200 hours (www.jetadvisors.com). Aircraft usage will be increased between inspection intervals, due to the aircraft engines remaining turned off during ground taxi under electric power.

When the TFE731-5B engine is operated during taxi at a 7 percent thrust, a typical twenty-six-minute ground taxi will generate 9.11 g/kg hydrocarbons, 47.70 g/kg of CO_2, and 3.12 g/kg of nitrogen oxides (times two engines). This is also known as the carbon footprint. This will be eliminated when the aircraft is using electrical power for ground taxi operations (see **Appendix E**).

Hawker Beechcraft Hawker 800A

The Hawker 800A was the first of the 800 series, which by now includes the Hawker 800SP, 800XP, 800XPi, and 850XP. The private jets of the 800 series are among the most popular in the private jet industry and continue to meet the high performance standards they are known for. The most well-known member of the 800 series is the Hawker 800XP.

The Hawker 800A has winglets; the 800XP does not. The winglets add stability, especially in turbulent weather, but the smooth wing of the 800XP creates less drag and allows it to cruise faster and burn less fuel. The slightly slower speed of the Hawker 800A is due to its slightly less powerful engines: it uses two AlliedSignal TFE731-5R-1H engines, each capable of giving off 4,200 pounds of thrust on takeoff. While this is roughly 400 pounds less thrust than the 800XP, it is still quite sufficient for a private jet of its size (www.jetadvisors.com).

When the TFE731-5R-1H engine is operated during taxi at a 7 percent thrust, a typical twenty-six-minute ground taxi will generate 8.89 g/kg hydrocarbons, 43.60 g/kg of CO_2, and 2.99 g/kg of nitrogen oxides (times two engines). This is also known as the carbon footprint. This will be eliminated when the aircraft is using electrical power for ground taxi operations (see **Appendix F**).

Hawker Beechcraft Hawker 800XP

The Hawker 800XP is one of the most successful private jets that British Aerospace has ever made. It is a third-generation model of the 800 series and is similar in part to the ubiquitous Hawker 400XP. It is designed to complete transcontinental and international flights as needed, to have good short-range capabilities. Since it is the third member of the 800 series, it has undergone many small improvements to the features that made it successful in the private jet market to begin with—its cruise and climb speeds, runway performance, and weight limits.

Two AlliedSignal TFE731-5BR engines power the Hawker 800XP, capable of giving off 4,660 pounds of thrust each on takeoff. The Hawker 800XP can climb to an altitude of 37,000 feet in twenty minutes, where it can reach its high cruise speed of 447 knots. For long-range cruise speeds, the Hawker 800XP flies at 39,000 feet at a speed of 400 knots. If needed, it can fly up to 41,000 feet to avoid traffic or weather. The cabin is pressurized to 8.6 psi, meaning that it can maintain a sea-level cabin at 22,200 feet (www.jetadvisors.com).

When the TFE731-5BR engine is operated during taxi at a 7 percent thrust, a typical twenty-six-minute ground taxi will generate 8.88 g/kg hydrocarbons, 43.70 g/kg of CO_2, and 2.96 g/kg of nitrogen oxides (times two engines). This is also known as the carbon footprint. This will be eliminated when the aircraft is using electrical power for ground taxi operations (see **Appendix G**).

Hawker Beechcraft Hawker 850XP

The Hawker family has mastered the art of evolution. Designed with the latest improvements in technology, the Hawker 850XP climbs faster, goes farther, and performs better than its predecessor, the successful 800XP. Certified in 2006, the 850XP's greatest feature is its design, more specifically the addition of winglets.

The slight modification improves overall performance by creating a more aerodynamic aircraft. The 850XP climbs to 39,000 feet two minutes faster than its predecessor and can travel an additional 100 nautical miles. It completes cross-country trips such as Teterboro to San Francisco (2,225 nm). Less drag means that the aircraft is capable of traveling against headwinds at a high-speed cruise of

448 kta and requires less fuel. Surprisingly, winglets also increase the aircraft's basic inspection interval from 300 to 600 hours. Two AlliedSignal TFE731-5BR engines power the Hawker 800XP, capable of giving off 4,660 pounds of thrust each on takeoff (www.jetadvisors.com).

When the TFE731-5BR engine is operated during taxi at a 7 percent thrust, a typical twenty-six-minute ground taxi will generate 8.88 g/kg hydrocarbons, 43.70 g/kg of CO_2, and 2.96 g/kg of nitrogen oxides (times two engines). This is also known as the carbon footprint. This will be eliminated when the aircraft is using electrical power for ground taxi operations (see **Appendix G**).

Hawker Beechcraft Hawker 900XP

Evolution is what makes Hawker aircraft so successful. In 2006, the midsize 850XP made significant improvements in performance and accommodations. True to form, the 900XP retains all of the 850's advanced traits (fuel efficiency, aerodynamics, comfort, performance capabilities) but makes them better. The long-range business jet features an enhanced variation of the 850XP's winglets, increasing hot/high-altitude and cruise performance and range.

On the runway in hot/high conditions, the 900XP requires 1,800 feet less runway for a 2,000-nautical-mile trip with six passengers. It can complete coast-to-coast trips, Teterboro to Seattle, for example. The 900XP features Honeywell TFE731-50R engines designed specifically for the aircraft. Each is rated at 4,660 pounds of thrust. Increased climb performance and immediate maximum altitude (41,000 feet) are benefits of the new engines (www.jetadvisors.com).

When the TFE731 50R engine is operated during taxi at a 7 percent thrust, a typical twenty-six-minute ground taxi will generate 8.89 g/kg hydrocarbons, 43.60 g/kg of CO_2, and 2.97 g/kg of nitrogen oxides (times two engines). This is also known as the carbon footprint. This will be eliminated when the aircraft is using electrical power for ground taxi operations (see **Appendix H**).

Gates Learjet 55

The Lear family is one of the pioneers of private jet aviation. Learjets have brought performance and innovation to the aviation market, starting with the original Learjet 23 in 1963. Introduced in 1981, the Learjet 55 incorporates successful elements of former Learjets, while adding a few design modifications of its own, like a larger fuselage. Although its predecessors were competitive, Lear essentially produced the 55 to contend in a growing business aircraft market, namely one with greater cabin accommodations.

The midsize cabin aircraft is the perfect combination of the 30-series' turbofan engines and the 20-series' "Longhorn" wing. Lear began replacing turbojet engines with turbofans starting with the Learjet 35 in 1974. A pair of TFE731-3A-2B engines powers the Learjet 55, providing 3,700 pounds of thrust apiece. Inspection interval is 4,200 hours. Adapted from the 28 and 29 Longhorn models, the Learjet 55 features an increased wingspan and drag-reducing winglets using higher-strength aluminum (www. jetadvisors.com).

When the TFE731-3A-2B engine is operated during taxi at a 7 percent thrust, a typical twenty-six-minute ground taxi will generate 8.80 g/kg hydrocarbons, 43.59 g/kg of CO_2, and 2.99 g/kg of nitrogen oxides (times two engines). This is also known as the carbon footprint. This will be eliminated when the aircraft is using electrical power for ground taxi operations (see **Appendix I**).

Bombardier Learjet 60

The Learjet 60 is said to have been designed for a niche market—private jets that can climb quickly to high cruise levels, have fast cruise speeds, operate economically, and are reliable.

The strongest feature of the Learjet 60 is its cruise performance. It can climb to its cruise level of 43,000 feet in less than fourteen minutes when loaded to its maximum takeoff weight of 23,500 pounds. Once at cruise level, it can reach speeds of up to 457 knots (about .76 Mach). It has a transcontinental range of 2,590 miles (2,250 nautical miles) when carrying six or seven passengers.

With an average fuel consumption of 203 gallons per hour, the 60 is surprisingly comparable to smaller lightweight private jets. A large contributing factor to Lear 60's speed is its aerodynamic design. For the first time in a Learjet, the NASA/Boeing Tranair computational fluid dynamics (CFD) software was used; the software locates points on the jet that cause excessive drag, resulting in a 4 percent reduction in overall drag. Pratt & Whitney Canada supplied the engines for the Learjet 60: two PW305A turbofans. They are flat-rated to 4,600 pounds of thrust each to reduce takeoff noise but have the capacity to provide 5,225 pounds of thrust (www.jetadvisors.com).

When the PW305A engine is operated during taxi at a 7 percent thrust, a typical twenty-six-minute ground taxi will generate 50.10 g/kg hydrocarbons, 130.01 g/kg of CO_2, and 1.65 g/kg of nitrogen oxides (times two engines). This is also known as the carbon footprint. This will be eliminated when the aircraft is using electrical power for ground taxi operations (see **Appendix J**).

Bombardier Learjet 60XR

Bombardier's midsize Learjet 60XR is the last iteration of the legacy of Learjets. This legacy derives from a long line of aircraft developed by Bill Lear in 1963, beginning with the original Learjet 23. The 60XR rounds out Learjet's generation of turbofan-powered aircraft. It is an improved version of the 60, with a more space-efficient interior. The redesigned model took its first flight in early 2006, and it remains a strong competitor in the medium-range business jet category. Based on the large-cabin 55 series, the Learjet 60XR increased in size and performance value. It is the first of the line to use PW305 turbofan engines instead of General Electric engine models. The Pratt & Whitney Canada PWC305A engines have 4,600 pounds of thrust each. They have an inspection interval of 6,000 hours (www.jetadvisors.com).

When the PW305A engine is operated during taxi at a 7 percent thrust, a typical twenty-six-minute ground taxi will generate 50.10 g/kg hydrocarbons, 130.01 g/kg of CO_2, and 1.65 g/kg of nitrogen oxides (times two engines). This is also known as the carbon footprint. This will be eliminated when the aircraft is using electrical power for ground taxi operations (see **Appendix J**).

Dassault Falcon 900

The Falcon 900 was Dassault's first foray into the heavy-iron private jet market. This is not to say that Dassault is an inexperienced company, by any means—their jets are known for having high standards of engineering, structural quality, and technological advancement—but the Falcon 900 was a step beyond where they had gone before. The cabin of the Falcon 900 is huge. It is 6.2 feet high, 7.7 feet wide, thirty-nine feet long (not including the cockpit), and has a total volume of 1,267 cubic feet. Standard seating is between eight and twelve passengers in a double-club configuration with a three-person divan.

The Falcon 900 can take off in 5,300 feet at sea level (or at 8,095 feet at an altitude of 5,000 feet and a temperature of 77° F) due in part to its three (not two) Honeywell TFE731-5AR-1C engines. They are flat-rated to 4,500 pounds of thrust apiece. The Falcon 900's short runway performance is also attributable to its very light, tough frame. It is made of titanium, Kevlar, and carbon fiber composites, all of which are very lightweight but sturdy materials that allow the Falcon to do what much heavier private jets with more powerful engines can (www. jetadvisors.com).

When the TFE731-5AR-1C engine is operated during taxi at a 7 percent thrust, a typical twenty-six-minute ground taxi will generate 8.90 g/kg hydrocarbons, 44.45 g/kg of CO_2, and 2.98 g/kg of nitrogen oxides (times three engines). This is also known as the carbon footprint. This will be eliminated when the aircraft is using electrical power for ground taxi operations (see **Appendix K**).

Bombardier Challenger 600

The Challenger 600 is more like an airliner than a private jet. Comparable to the Boeing 737, it offers much more cabin space than any similar aircraft. It is quiet, fairly economical, and handles well. Pilots love to fly it, and passengers love the spacious, comfortable cabin and transcontinental range.

It's a very roomy private jet. Two Avco Lycoming ALF502L engines power the Challenger 600. They were modified to add supercharger stages to the low-pressure compressor, enabling more than 7,500 pounds of thrust on takeoff. The Challenger 600 can take off in 5,700 feet at sea level or in 7,350 feet at 5,000 feet at a temperature of 77° F (www.jetadvisors.com).

When the Avco Lycoming ALF502L engine is operated during taxi at a 7 percent thrust, a typical twenty-six-minute ground taxi will generate 0.94 g/kg hydrocarbons,

29.28 g/kg of CO_2, and 3.91 g/kg of nitrogen oxides (times two engines). This is also known as the carbon footprint. This will be eliminated when the aircraft is using electrical power for ground taxi operations (see **Appendix L**).

Bombardier Challenger 601-1A

Bombardier designed the original Challenger 601 with the primary goal of passenger comfort. It is unusually wide-bodied and can carry up to nineteen passengers in its 8.2 foot wide cabin, yet it has transcontinental range and is able to complete nonstop flights between almost any two cities in the United States. The 601 series has improved immensely over the 600, with a more reliable flight system and increased maintainability. The 601-1A iteration signifies the use of General Electric CF43-1A engines and drag-reducing winglets.

Two General Electric CF43-1A engines power the Challenger 601-1A, each flat-rated to 70° F, meaning that the engines provide their full 8,650 pounds of thrust in temperatures up to 70° F. Performance drops slightly above the 70° mark, but they still perform well in temperatures over 90° F. The Challenger 601-1A can take off in 5,400 feet (at sea level) with an increased takeoff weight of 44,600 pounds. It can take five passengers up to 3,500 nautical miles nonstop (www.jetadvisors.com).

When the General Electric CF43-1A engine is operated during taxi at a 7 percent thrust setting, a typical twenty-six-minute ground taxi will generate 4.10 g/kg hydrocarbons, 40.71 g/kg of CO_2, and 3.71 g/kg of nitrogen oxides (times two engines). This is also known as the carbon footprint. This will be eliminated when the aircraft is using electrical power for ground taxi operations (see **Appendix M**).

Bombardier Challenger 601-3A

The Challenger 601-3A long-range business jet has made leaps and bounds since the original Challenger 600. With better-performing engines, greater range, and increased reliability, the 3A variant offers plenty of desirable qualities in its class, even two decades later. The 3A's single greatest improvement is its General Electric CF24-3A high-bypass engines. Each engine is rated at a considerable 8,650 pounds of thrust at takeoff, while the inspection interval is 6,000 hours. As a result, the 601-3A is capable of traveling 3,290 nautical miles in one trip and at .85 Mach (www.jetadvisors.com).

When the General Electric CF24-3 engine is operated during taxi at a 7 percent thrust, a typical twenty-six-minute ground taxi will generate 3.99 g/kg hydrocarbons, 38.71 g/kg of CO_2, and 3.88 g/kg of nitrogen oxides (times two engines). This is also known as the carbon footprint. This will be eliminated when the aircraft is using electrical power for ground taxi operations (see **Appendix N**).

Bombardier Challenger 601-3R

A derivative of the Challenger 600, the Challenger 601 was designed with the primary goal of passenger comfort. It is unusually wide-bodied and can carry up to nineteen passengers in its 8.2-foot-wide cabin, yet it has transcontinental range and is able to complete nonstop flights between almost any two cities in the United States. Its flight systems are reliable, and it is generally very easy to maintain. The 601 series includes two variations: the 601-3A and 601-3R. Sharing everything but the engine, a t-tail, and tail cone fuel tank, the 601-3R is the most recent variation and replaced the 3A in 1993.

As previously mentioned, the cabin of this private jet is uncharacteristically large. Two General Electric CF34-3A1 engines power the Challenger 601-3R, each flat-rated to 70° F, meaning that the engines provide their full 8,729 pounds of thrust (seventy-nine more than the 601) in temperatures up to 70° F. Performance drops slightly above the 70° mark, but they still perform well in temperatures over 90° F. The Challenger 601-3R can take off in 6,050 feet (at sea level) and has a cruise speed of 460 knots. It can take five passengers up to 3,585 nautical miles nonstop (www.jetadvisors.com).

When the General Electric CF34-3A1 engine is operated during taxi at a 7 percent thrust setting, a typical twenty-six-minute ground taxi will generate 4.01 g/kg hydrocarbons, 41.79 g/kg of CO_2, and 3.60 g/kg of nitrogen oxides (times two engines). This is also known as the carbon footprint. This will be eliminated when the aircraft is using electrical power for ground taxi operations (see **Appendix O**).

Bombardier Challenger 604

Beginning with the original Challenger 600, Bombardier created a successful family of business jets. After numerous refinements and upgrades, the Challenger 604 secures the family name in the long-range, business jet market. Certified in 1995, the 604 provides range, speed, and sophistication and style. A lot of power can be found in the Challenger 604. Two General Electric CF34-3B engines propel the jet, each rated at 8,729 pounds of thrust. This means that with eight passengers, the 604 can fly 3,850 miles and at .74 Mach. However, 4,000+ nautical mile legs are possible at 424 kta (a personal milestone for Canadair) due to new fuel distribution and greater capacity of 2,460 gallons (www.jetadvisors.com).

When the General Electric CF34-3B engine is operated during taxi at a 7 percent thrust, a typical twenty-six-minute ground taxi will generate 3.99 g/kg hydrocarbons, 41.70 g/kg of CO_2, and 3.65 g/kg of nitrogen oxides (times two engines). This is also known as the carbon footprint. This will be eliminated when the aircraft is using electrical power for ground taxi operations (see **Appendix P**).

Bombardier Challenger 605

Bombardier's Challenger series, perhaps its most successful line, has only become better with experience. Because the original Challenger was so successful, Bombardier continues to use its general design while incorporating up-to-date technology and improvements on well-received components. It would be a challenge, pun intended, to fill the shoes of the Challenger 604, the "best-selling model in the heavy-iron category." However, the Challenger 605 maintains every praised feature of its predecessor, adding freedom, innovation, and performance capabilities. It's no wonder that this $27 million long-range business jet is a valuable asset to corporate clients.

Bombardier chose to preserve the spacious "Challenger" cabin that has accommodated business travelers for years. Overall, the Challenger 605's cabin offers more in every respect. Two General Electric CF34-3B engines propel the jet, each rated at 8,729 pounds of thrust (www.jetadvisors.com).

When the General Electric CF34-3B engine is operated during taxi at a 7 percent thrust setting, a typical twenty-six-minute ground taxi will generate 3.99 g/kg hydrocarbons, 41.70 g/kg of CO_2, and 3.65 g/kg of nitrogen oxides (times two engines). This is also known as the carbon footprint. This will be eliminated when the aircraft is using electrical power for ground taxi operations (see **Appendix P**).

Dassault Falcon

The Falcon 2000 is a private jet with a large cabin, transcontinental range, and fast cruise speeds. It can easily complete nonstop flights such as trips from Miami to Seattle or from Boston to San Francisco. The cabin of the Dassault Falcon 2000 has a volume of 1,024 cubic feet and usually seats between eight and twelve passengers.

Two CFE738 axial-centrifugal flow engines supply the power for the Falcon 2000EX. They provide 5,918 pounds of thrust apiece and are flat-rated to improve runway performance at high altitudes and temperatures. At sea level, the Falcon 2000 can take off in 5,436 feet but needs 7,656 feet of runway at an altitude of 5,000 feet and a temperature of 77° F (www.jetadvisors.com).

When the General Electric CFE738 engine is operated during taxi at a 7 percent thrust, a typical twenty-six-minute ground taxi will generate 3.98 g/kg hydrocarbons, 40.70 g/kg of CO_2, and 3.85 g/kg of nitrogen oxides (times two engines). This is also known as the carbon footprint. This will be eliminated when the aircraft is using electrical power for ground taxi operations (see **Appendix Q**).

Dassault Falcon 2000DX

High standards of engineering, structural quality, and technological advancement are at the forefront of the Dassault family thinking. The Falcon 900 series has been one of Dassault's best-performing aircraft. It was certified in 1995 and has since produced upgraded variations, including the Falcon 2000DX, EX, and the latest, LX. The first upgrade, the Falcon 2000DX, maintains the design and systems of the original 2000 but is a better-performing aircraft overall.

The Falcon 2000DX comes equipped with two Pratt & Whitney Canada PW308C engines, rated at 7,000 of thrust each. For optimal performance and convenience, the engines are controlled by dual FADECs (Full Authority

Digital Engine Control), and three LCD screens display engine parameters. Their inspection interval is 7,000 hours (www.jetadvisors.com).

When the Pratt & Whitney Canada PW308C engine is operated during taxi at a 7 percent thrust, a typical twenty-six-minute ground taxi will generate 49.02 g/kg hydrocarbons, 12.01 g/kg of CO_2, and 1.61 g/kg of nitrogen oxides (times two engines). This is also known as the carbon footprint. This will be eliminated when the aircraft is using electrical power for ground taxi operations (see **Appendix R**).

Dassault Falcon 2000EX EASY

Eight years after the release of the successful Falcon 2000, Dassault released the Falcon 2000EX. It still had all of the components that made the Falcon 2000 great—economy, speed, a large cabin—but improved on all of these elements to make an even better jet. The cabin of the Dassault Falcon 2000EX has a volume of more than 1,000 cubic feet and usually seats between eight and twelve passengers.

Two Pratt & Whitney Canada PW308C engines supply the power for the Falcon 2000EX. They provide 7,000 pounds of thrust apiece (1,800 more than the Falcon 2000). At sea level, the Falcon 2000EX can take off in 5,585 feet but needs 8,120 feet of runway at an altitude of 5,000 feet and a temperature of 77° F. Even though the Falcon 2000EX has a fuel capacity that is 3,800 pounds heavier than the Falcon 2000, it still manages to be just as economical as its predecessor but with a greater range, due largely to the more advanced technology of the Pratt & Whitney Canada engines (www.jetadvisors.com).

When the Pratt & Whitney Canada PW308C engine is operated during taxi at a 7 percent thrust, a typical twenty-six-minute ground taxi will generate 49.02 g/kg hydrocarbons, 12.01 g/kg of CO_2, and 1.61 g/kg of nitrogen oxides (times two engines). This is also known as the carbon footprint. This will be eliminated when the aircraft is using electrical power for ground taxi operations (see **Appendix R**).

Dassault Falcon 2000LX

Over a decade after the release of the successful Falcon 2000, Dassault released the Falcon 2000LX. It still has all of the components that made the Falcon 2000 series great—economy, speed, a large cabin—but improved on all of these elements to make an even better jet. The long-range Falcon 2000LX, essentially the EX model with the addition of winglets, is the most advanced and up-to-date aircraft in the series. The Falcon 2000 series is a reduced-size, twin-engine version of the popular 900 line. Dassault claimed a niche in the aircraft market when it introduced the original 2000 as a wide-body jet.

The 2000 aircraft has the same wide fuselage as the 900 but six feet shorter and with shorter range. Dassault received certification of the first Falcon 2000 in 1995, while the LX derivative was certified just last year. The 2000LX features modified wings and blended winglets, which allow increased climb performance and range. The Falcon 2000LX's biggest advantage over competitors and even predecessors is its application of winglets to the design frame. While the LX enjoys the same airfoil wing and span increase of the EX, engineers increased it even more to make room for the winglets.

Designed by Aviation Partners, the winglets alone increase the LX's range by 200 nautical miles from the EX. The 2000LX can cover 4,000 nautical miles, with eight passengers, on the same amount of fuel and thrust that it takes the EX to cover 3,800 nm. Winglets also allow the jet to climb directly to FL410 in a fleeting eighteen minutes. For one minor modification, these numbers are significant. The rest of the jet maintains the same components of the Falcon 2000 series that make it such a success.

Two Pratt & Whitney Canada PW308C engines supply the power for the Falcon 2000LX. They provide 7,000 pounds of thrust apiece (1,800 more than the Falcon 2000). At sea level, the Falcon 2000EX can take off in 5,585 feet but needs 8,120 feet of runway at an altitude of 5,000 feet and a temperature of 77° F. It has a tall certified flight ceiling of 47,000 feet. The 2000LX, like its predecessor, is able to fly at a high-speed cruise of 482 knots at an altitude of 39,000 feet (www.jetadvisors.com).

When the Pratt & Whitney Canada PW308C engine is operated during taxi at a 7 percent thrust, a typical twenty-six-minute ground taxi will generate 49.02 g/kg hydrocarbons, 12.01 g/kg of CO_2, and 1.61 g/kg of nitrogen oxides (times two engines). This is also known as the carbon footprint. This will be eliminated when the aircraft is using electrical power for ground taxi operations (see **Appendix R**).

Dassault Falcon 900

The Falcon 900 was Dassault's first foray into the heavy-iron private jet market. This is not to say that Dassault is an inexperienced company, by any means—their jets are known for having high standards of engineering, structural quality, and technological advancement—but the Falcon 900 was a step beyond where they had gone before. The cabin of the Falcon 900 is huge. It is 6.2 feet high, 7.7 feet wide, and thirty-nine feet long (not including the cockpit) and has a total volume of 1,267 cubic feet. Standard seating is between eight and twelve passengers in a double-club configuration with a three-person divan.

Two seats can be reclined and combined to make a full-length bed. Otherwise all of the seats are fully adjustable and can move along a track, swivel, recline, and do everything else a seat could feasibly do. Console tables come standard, and there is room for virtually any piece of equipment—computer, copier, scanner, TV, desk, and so on. Even with the tables and seats, there is plenty of room to walk around the cabin. The full-sized galley can be configured with equipment for hot meal preparation, including a high-temperature oven, a microwave, and the ubiquitous coffeemaker.

There are many interior configuration options, from wheelchair access to partitioned rooms. These separate rooms have been used to create a private office (with a full-sized desk) or a bedroom (with a queen-sized bed). The aft baggage compartment, which holds 127 cubic feet of baggage, is pressurized and air-conditioned and can be accessed in-flight. Sound levels within the cabin are very low, and temperature distribution is even throughout all parts of the cabin. The Falcon 900 can take off in 5,300 feet at sea level (or at 8,095 feet at an altitude of 5,000 feet and a temperature of 77° F), due in part to its three Honeywell TFE731-5AR-1C engines.

The Honeywell TFE731-5AR-1C engines are flat-rated to 4,500 pounds of thrust apiece. The Falcon 900's short runway performance is also attributable to its very light, tough frame. It is made of titanium, Kevlar, and carbon fiber composites, all of which are very lightweight but sturdy materials that allow the Falcon to do what much heavier private jets with more powerful engines can (www.jetadvisors.com).

When the Honeywell TFE731-5AR-1C engine is operated during taxi at a 7 percent thrust, a typical twenty-six-minute ground taxi will generate 8.90 g/kg hydrocarbons, 44.45 g/kg of CO_2, and 2.98 g/kg of nitrogen oxides (times three engines). This is also known as the carbon footprint. This will be eliminated when the aircraft is using electrical power for ground taxi operations (see **Appendix K**).

Dassault Falcon 900B

The Dassault family creates jets with high standards of engineering, structural quality, and technological advancement. Dassault is constantly redesigning and improving their aircraft to uphold these standards. In the intercontinental business jet category, the tri-jet Falcon 900s excel. Certified in 1992, the Falcon 900B iteration derives from its eight-year-old predecessor, the original Falcon 900. The "B" refers to upgraded engines, producing more power and performance capacity. It was so successful that 900s can be retrofitted to 900B capabilities.

Improvements from the 900 include a 5.5 percent increase in takeoff thrust, a 6.5 percent increase in thrust at altitude, and a 2 percent increase in TSFC (Thrust Specific Fuel Consumption). An increase in range is the result: 4,583 nautical miles. The 900B can also enjoy better visibility approach clearance (Category II) and operation on unprepared strips that its predecessor cannot.

The 900B has three AlliedSignal TFE731-5BR turbofan engines, each with 4,750 pounds of thrust. Their inspection interval is 4,200 hours. The aircraft can travel 3,995 nautical miles at as high as .84 Mach. Its high-speed cruise is 474 knots, and 51,000 feet is its flight ceiling, a rare feat. Also, the 900B is designed with airfoil wings—the same as the Falcon 50 series but with a 1.5-foot increase (www.jetadvisors.com).

When the Honeywell TFE731-5BR engine is operated during taxi at a 7 percent thrust, a typical twenty-six-minute ground taxi will generate 8.88 g/kg hydrocarbons,

43.70 g/kg of CO_2, and 2.96 g/kg of nitrogen oxides (times three engines). This is also known as the carbon footprint. This will be eliminated when the aircraft is using electrical power for ground taxi operations (see **Appendix G**).

Dassault Falcon 900C

The Dassault family creates jets with high standards of engineering, structural quality, and technological advancement. Dassault is constantly redesigning and improving their aircraft to uphold these standards. In the intercontinental business jet category, the tri-jet Falcon 900s excel. Introduced in 2000, the Falcon 900C is the sculpted, evolved version of its predecessor, the original Falcon 900, combining the 900B's improvements with the innovative avionics of the 900EX.

Improvements made in the 900B that the newer variant maintains are a 5.5 percent increase in takeoff thrust, a 6.5 percent increase in thrust at altitude, and a 2 percent increase in TSFC (Thrust Specific Fuel Consumption), resulting in an increase in range to 4,583 nautical miles. The aircraft also enjoys better visibility approach clearance (Category II) and operation on unprepared strips that its original predecessor cannot.

The 900C is powered by three AlliedSignal TFE731-5BR-1C turbofan engines, each with 4,750 pounds of thrust. Their inspection interval is 4,200 hours. The aircraft can travel 3,995 nautical miles at as high as .84 Mach. Its high-speed cruise is 474 knots, and 51,000 feet is its flight ceiling (www.jetadvisors.com).

When the Honeywell TFE731-5BR-1C engine is operated during taxi at a 7 percent thrust, a typical twenty-six-minute ground taxi will generate 8.90 g/kg hydrocarbons, 44.45 g/kg of CO_2, and 2.98 g/kg of nitrogen oxides (times three engines). This is also known as the carbon footprint. This will be eliminated when the aircraft is using electrical power for ground taxi operations (see **Appendix S**).

Dassault Falcon 900DX

With forty-four years in the industry, Dassault-Aviation's Falcon family is comprised of highly reputable, two- or three-engine business jets. Evolved from the original long-range Falcon 900, the Falcon 900DX is just one step down from the top-performing EX. Offering all but a few of the EX's competitive performance capabilities, the Falcon 900DX is a value at under $35 million. The Falcon 900DX was introduced in 2005 and continues to be manufactured today.

Dassault modified the design of the former Falcon 900s to create a more reliable, better-performing aircraft.

The frame is almost entirely constructed of carbon fiber and Kevlar (featured specifically in the tail cone, radome, and cabin doors). The Falcon 900DX has a lower takeoff speed, placing more thrust accumulation near the centerline. It can climb to its initial cruise altitude (FL370) in just seventeen minutes, one minute faster than the superior EX, and travel 4,000 nautical miles. The DX's high-speed cruise is 474 knots, and its flight ceiling is a substantial 51,000 feet. It gains in runway requirements as an exchange for a lower maximum takeoff weight (www. jetadvisors.com).

When the Honeywell TFE731-5BR engine is operated during taxi at a 7 percent thrust, a typical twenty-six-minute ground taxi will generate 8.88 g/kg hydrocarbons, 43.70 g/kg of CO_2, and 2.96 g/kg of nitrogen oxides (times three engines). This is also known as the carbon footprint. This will be eliminated when the aircraft is using electrical power for ground taxi operations (see **Appendix G**).

Dassault Falcon 900EX

Dassault, a company known for having high standards of engineering, structural quality, and technological advancement, made an impact on the heavy-iron private jet market with the Falcon 900. Ten years later, they improved an already great private jet and introduced the Falcon 900EX. The cabin of the Falcon 900EX is huge. It is 6.1 feet high, 7.7 feet wide, thirty-nine feet long (not including the cockpit), and has a total volume of 1,264 cubic feet.

Standard seating is between eight and twelve passengers in a double-club configuration and a three-person divan. Two seats can be reclined and combined to make a full-length bed. Otherwise, all of the seats are fully adjustable and can move along a track, swivel, recline, and do everything else a seat could feasibly do. Console tables come standard, and there is room for virtually any piece of equipment—computer, copier, scanner, TV, desk, and so on. Even with the tables and seats, there is plenty of room to walk around the cabin.

The aft baggage compartment, which holds 127 cubic feet of baggage, is pressurized and air-conditioned and can be accessed in-flight. Sound levels within the cabin are very low, and temperature distribution is even throughout all parts of the cabin. The Falcon 900EX can take off in 5,213 feet at sea level (or at 7,214 feet at an altitude of 5,000 feet and a temperature of 77° F) due in part to its three Honeywell TFE731-60 engines. The Honeywell TFE731-60 engines are flat-rated to 5,000 pounds of thrust apiece, 500 pounds more than the Falcon 900 (www.jetadvisors.com).

When the Honeywell TFE731-60 engine is operated during taxi at a 7 percent thrust, a typical twenty-six-minute ground taxi will generate 8.60 g/kg hydrocarbons, 41.10 g/kg of CO_2, and 3.11 g/kg of nitrogen oxides (times two engines). This is also known as the carbon footprint. This will be eliminated when the aircraft is using electrical power for ground taxi operations (see **Appendix T**).

Gulfstream GII

Today, Gulfstream jets are used as a model for comparing large executive aircraft. The Gulfstream II is the quintessential example of a transcontinental-range jet that has stood alone in its class. After manufacturing the original Gulfstream I turboprop executive jet, Gulfstream tore it apart and started from the ground up. The GII was introduced in 1965, completely altered and enhanced. The Gulfstream II bears very little resemble to its predecessor, the Gulfstream I. In fact, the only remnant of the original is the large fuselage cross-section. The GII has upgraded engines, new swept wings, and a stand-up cabin. The GII is powered by two Rolls-Royce Spey Mk 511-8 engines, each rated at 11,400 pounds of thrust. A large powerhouse is needed to complete the G-II's transcontinental range capabilities. The inspection interval is 8,000 hours. The first GII featured swept wings, a much more aerodynamic alternative to the original Gulfstream I. In later variants, tip-tanks were added to the wings, allowing 4,000 more pounds of fuel capacity, increasing the range to 3,329 nautical miles (www.jetadvisors.com).

When the Rolls-Royce Spey Mk 511-8 engine is operated during taxi at a 7 percent thrust, a typical twenty-six-minute ground taxi will generate 3.42 g/kg hydrocarbons, 39.91 g/kg of CO_2, and 3.99 g/kg of nitrogen oxides (times two engines). This is also known as the carbon footprint. This will be eliminated when the aircraft is using electrical power for ground taxi operations (see **Appendix U**).

Gulfstream GIIB

The Gulfstream GIIB is one of the elite large-cabin global private jets. It was designed for optimal range, runway performance, and flight performance. Since its release to the market, it has become one of the most-used private jets in the business world; companies like IBM and General Motors purchased more than one GII, and Coca-Cola purchased four. The Gulfstream GIIB has intercontinental range and is truly an international jet. Its owners routinely take trips around the world to every destination imaginable: New York, Tel Aviv, Djokjakarta, Perth, Bora Bora, Sydney. The GIIB can go everywhere.

Power for the GIIB is provided by two Rolls-Royce Spey Mk 511-8 engines, which provide 11,400 pounds of thrust each on takeoff. The GIIB climbs at a rate of 4,350 feet per minute. It can fly as fast as 488 knots or at 442 knots for maximum range. The GIIB can fly up to 4,276 miles (3,714 nautical miles) with maximum fuel and reserves. Its maximum flight ceiling is 45,000 feet. The cabin of the GIIB is huge: a total of 1,270 cubic feet. The cabin is usually configured to hold ten to fourteen passengers but can be configured to hold as many as nineteen. The cabin of the GIIB is 6.1 feet high, 7.3 feet wide, and 33.9 feet long. At the time of its release, it had the largest cabin of any private jet available. Both a large entertainment center and a galley are included (www.jetadvisors.com).

When the Rolls-Royce Spey Mk 511-8 engine is operated during taxi at a 7 percent thrust, a typical twenty-six-minute ground taxi will generate 3.42 g/kg hydrocarbons, 39.91 g/kg of CO_2, and 3.99 g/kg of nitrogen oxides (times two engines). This is also known as the carbon footprint. This will be eliminated when the aircraft is using electrical power for ground taxi operations (see **Appendix U**).

Gulfstream GIII

The Gulfstream GIII is the third generation of a very successful family line of private jets. Gulfstream Aerospace Corp designed the Gulfstream GIII to be similar to the GII (of which more than 250 models were sold) but better. The GIII can fly 4,600 miles (4,000 nautical miles) at a speed of .84 Mach while carrying eight passengers. Alternately, it can fly 4,140 miles (3,600 nautical miles) at the same speed with twice the number of passengers. The cabin of the GIII usually holds fourteen to nineteen passengers, but it can be configured to hold up to nineteen in a high-density layout. The cabin has sufficiently spacious dimensions: 41.3 feet long, 6.1 feet high, and 7.3 feet wide, totaling a cabin volume of 1,345 cubic feet. Standard amenities include a full-sized galley with a refrigerator, coffeemaker, and the usual food preparation equipment.

The choice to use two Rolls-Royce Spey Mk 511-8 engines, the exact engines used on the GII, was not made by default. Before deciding on the two-engine configuration, Gulfstream Aerospace Corp tested three- and four-engine configurations. In the end, they decided that two engines would provide the performance capabilities for the jet while keeping costs low.

Each engine is able to produce 11,400 pounds of thrust each on takeoff, but the two are flat-rated to 9,000 pounds in order to meet FAR part 36 noise requirements. In the case of an engine failure, however, the remaining engine will automatically jump to full power (www.jetadvisors.com).

When the Rolls-Royce Spey Mk 511-8 engine is operated during taxi at a 7 percent thrust, a typical twenty six minute ground taxi will generate 3.42 g/kg hydrocarbons, 39.91 g/kg of CO_2, and 3.99 g/kg of nitrogen oxides (times two engines). This is also known as the carbon footprint. This will be eliminated when the aircraft is using electrical power for ground taxi operations (see **Appendix U**).

Embraer Legacy 600

The Legacy 600 is Embraer's first attempt at a business jet, but it doesn't show. Certified in 1999, the highly successful Legacy 600 continues to be manufactured today. Now the Legacy series, although still in development, is highly anticipated and promises the most up-to-date technology yet. The Legacy 600 is unmatched in its class in performance, operation, and interior size, to name just a few.

For optimal comfort and enjoyment, cabin amenities include two seventeen-inch flat-screen monitors, DVD players with individual controls, and posh seats that fully recline. Twenty-two large windows and full LED lighting make the cabin feel exceptionally spacious. A roomy, private lavatory is aft, while a second is optional (forward-positioned).

Embraer chose two Rolls-Royce AE3007A1E high-bypass, turbofan, dual FADEC engines for the Legacy 600. Each is rated at 7,987 pounds of thrust. This allows the 600 to travel 3,250 nautical miles at . 74 Mach carrying eight passengers. It has a high-speed cruise of 455 knots and a flight ceiling of 41,000 feet. It's obvious the engines can perform, but in addition, they are extremely quiet (13 dB below Stage IV requirements) and fuel-efficient (www. jetadvisors.com).

When the Rolls-Royce AE3007A1E high-bypass engine is operated during taxi at a 7 percent thrust, a typical twenty-six-minute ground taxi will generate 3.52 g/kg hydrocarbons, 37.97 g/kg of CO_2, and 4.26 g/kg of nitrogen oxides (times two engines). This is also known as the carbon footprint. This will be eliminated when the aircraft is using electrical power for ground taxi operations (see **Appendix V**).

Embraer Legacy Shuttle

The Embraer Legacy Shuttle began life as a highly successful commercial aircraft in 1999. Its parent company, Embraer, decided that their popular fifty-passenger commercial jet, the ERJ-135, would translate well into a thirteen-passenger private jet. The resulting aircraft was a cross between the ERJ-135 and 145 and was met with success in the private jet industry. Modified in several ways to meet the needs of corporate jet flyers, the jet retained most of its original design. Although the EMB-135 was the first of the Embraer private jets, it already boasted plenty of experience in the field.

The most notable modifications made to the EMB-135 were the addition of winglets (increasing speed and stability) and the addition of several auxiliary fuel tanks (increasing the jet's fuel capacity from 11,300 pounds to 18,160 pounds). Two years later, Embraer released the EMB-135LR, another model that has fared well since its debut in 2004.

The EMB-135LR, in contrast to its predecessor, is designed to work best on shorter trips. It can carry more passengers than its predecessor and is designed to be used as a corporate shuttle for anywhere between sixteen and thirty-seven passengers.

The Legacy Shuttle meets its design objectives very well. It is extremely practical, making it an ideal private jet for day-to-day business use. In addition, it is exceptionally reliable, retaining plenty of backup systems for each key function, as should be expected from a private jet originally designed for day-in, day-out commercial use.

The Legacy Shuttle is powered by two Rolls-Royce AE3007 A1/E turbofan engines. Each engine is flat-rated to 7,057 pounds of thrust. Inspection is on-condition. FADEC makes engine startup almost entirely automatic and regulates their performance in-flight for optimal fuel burn and speed. On average, the engines burn 313 gallons of fuel per hour. www.jetadvisors.com

When the Rolls-Royce AE3007A1E high-bypass engine is operated during taxi at a 7 percent thrust, a typical twenty-six-minute ground taxi will generate 3.52 g/kg hydrocarbons, 37.97 g/kg of CO_2, and 4.26 g/kg of nitrogen oxides (times two engines). This is also known as the carbon footprint. This will be eliminated when the aircraft is using electrical power for ground taxi operations (see **Appendix V**).

Bombardier Global 5000

At the time of the Global 5000's release, Bombardier called the Global 5000 "the world's fastest" ultra-long-range private jet. It is designed to be slightly smaller and faster than the Global Express, for those that value reliability and speed, without the extensive range capabilities of the Express. It can fly eight passengers and three crew members 4,800 nautical miles nonstop at a speed of .85 Mach. It is impressive in its speed, cabin size, and reliability.

Bombardier was anything but stingy in the design of the Global 5000's cabin. It usually holds eight passengers but is able to hold seventeen in a high-density configuration. The cabin measures 37.3 feet long, 8.2 feet wide, and 6.2 feet high—five feet shorter than the length of the Global Express. The total cabin volume is 1,881 cubic feet, and even though the cabin is significantly shorter than that of the Global Express, the passengers may not notice.

Most of the space reduction came from the crew rest and galley areas (the oversized galley of the Global Express was reduced to a full-sized one in the Global 5000). Only ten inches of space was taken from the main passenger area. Despite the decrease in fuselage length, the cabin still has plenty of room for cabin amenities and business equipment.

The Global 5000 is powered by two Rolls-Royce Deutschland BR710-20 turbofan engines. Each engine produces 14,750 pounds of thrust on takeoff, a performance standard that it can achieve in temperatures up to 95° F. The maximum range of the Global 5000, while flying at .85 Mach (488 knots), is 5,520 miles (4,800 nautical miles). Its high-speed cruise is .89 Mach, or 499 knots. Its takeoff range is exceptionally short: when loaded to its maximum takeoff weight of 87,700 pounds, it can take off in only 5,000 feet. The jet is able to climb to 43,000 feet in twenty-three minutes.

When the Rolls-Royce Deutschland BR710-20 engine is operated during taxi at a 7 percent thrust, a typical twenty-six-minute ground taxi will generate 3.99 g/kg hydrocarbons, 39.93 g/kg of CO_2, and 4.21 g/kg of nitrogen oxides (times two engines). This is also known as the carbon footprint. This will be eliminated when the aircraft is using electrical power for ground taxi operations (see **Appendix W**).

Bombardier Global Express

The Global Express was the pioneer of ultra-long-range private jets. At the time of its release, no other private jet had a cabin nearly as large, nor could any jet make such long-range direct flights like New York to Tokyo or Paris to Singapore. The Global Express offers everything an airliner does—range, comfort, and speed—without the hassle. The cabin of the Global Express is designed to offer maximum comfort and amenities for the duration of long, transoceanic flights. The cabin can be configured to hold between thirteen and nineteen passengers in a space that is 6.3 feet high, 8.2 feet wide, and 48.4 feet long. The cabin can be divided into three areas for increased privacy in conferences.

Two fully enclosed lavatories are located in the cabin, one of which can be equipped with a shower if desired. Extensive cabin insulation cuts down on noise, and improved engines produce less audible vibration. There is a wide range of standard and optional cabin amenities, including a seventeen-channel SATCOM, fax machine, and cabin entertainment system with VHS, DVD, and CD players, as well as individual video screens and a full-sized galley.

The engines themselves are BMW/Rolls-Royce BR710-20 turbofans, which produce 14,750 pounds of thrust each on takeoff. The Global Express can climb to 37,000 feet in nineteen minutes. Its maximum certified flight ceiling is 51,000 feet, but it generally cruises around 42,000 feet—well above most commercial and private jets. For long-distance flights, the Global Express can reach speeds of 488 knots and reach 499 knots when cruising at high speed.

When the Rolls-Royce Deutschland BR710-20 engine is operated during taxi at a 7 percent thrust, a typical twenty-six-minute ground taxi will generate 3.99 g/kg hydrocarbons, 39.93 g/kg of CO_2, and 4.21 g/kg of nitrogen oxides (times two engines). This is also known as the carbon footprint. This will be eliminated when the aircraft is using electrical power for ground taxi operations (see **Appendix W**).

Global Express XRS

The Global Express XRS is able to complete transcontinental and intercontinental flights due to its incredible powerhouse. The XRS gains this power from two Rolls-Royce Deutschland BR 10A2-20 turbofan engines. These engines produce 14,750 pounds of thrust each. Consequently, the XRS earns bragging rights with its 6,100+ nautical miles range.

The XRS is designed to travel at high speeds and high altitudes. Improved from its predecessor, the wing is swept back thirty-five degrees and features high-ratio root-to-tip taper and high aspect ratio. Four sections of aluminum slats also enable the aircraft to take off and land at lower speeds.

When the Rolls-Royce Deutschland BR710-20 engine is operated during taxi at a 7 percent thrust, a typical twenty-six-minute ground taxi will generate 3.99 g/kg hydrocarbons, 39.93 g/kg of CO_2, and 4.21 g/kg of nitrogen oxides (times two engines). This is also known as the carbon footprint. This will be eliminated when the aircraft is using electrical power for ground taxi operations (see **Appendix W**).

Gulfstream G350

The Gulfstream 350 is the next in line of business jet after the successful 300. However, the 350 is more similar in interior features, aerodynamic design, and advanced cockpit to its superior counterpart, the Gulfstream 450. The only difference between the jets is range: the 350's range is 3,797 nautical miles, while the 450's is 4,349 nm. The G350 is fitted with the Honeywell Primus Epic avionics suite.

The highly advanced PlaneView cockpit of the 450 is also found in the Gulfstream 350. It is comprised of four liquid crystal displays and the first Gulfstream Enhanced Vision System (EVS) with Honeywell 2020 Heads Up Display (HUD). With these advancements, pilots have greater situational awareness and safety. The G350 employs two Rolls-Royce Tay Mark 611-8C engines. Each engine produces 13,850 pounds of thrust. With this amount of power, the jet climbs to 37,000 feet in fifteen minutes, one minute faster than the 300. Its certified flight ceiling is 45,000 feet.

When the Rolls-Royce Tay Mark 611-8C engine is operated during taxi at a 7 percent thrust, a typical twenty-six-minute ground taxi will generate 2.98 g/kg hydrocarbons, 35.91 g/kg of CO_2, and 3.93 g/kg of nitrogen oxides (times two engines). This is also known as the carbon footprint. This will be eliminated when the aircraft is using electrical power for ground taxi operations (see **Appendix X**).

Gulfstream G450

The Gulfstream 400 has been a central figure in the large-cabin private jet lineup since its introduction to the market, and the Gulfstream 450 lives up to its standards. It can fly eight passengers and three crew members from Tokyo to Seattle at a speed of .80 Mach. Everything from its engines to its flight control systems is high-performing and reliable. Between fourteen and eighteen passengers should ride comfortably in the Gulfstream 450's 1,525-cubic-foot cabin. Passengers can easily stand in the 6.2-foot-high cabin and will enjoy the 7.3-foot width and 45.1-foot length (an eighteen-inch increase from the GIII). The 169 cubic feet of baggage space is accessible in-flight. Two full-length closets for coat storage are located inside the two fully enclosed lavatories.

There are plenty of cabin features that should make transcontinental and transoceanic flights enjoyable. To begin with, the full-sized galley comes equipped with everything needed for hot and cold food preparation: a high-temperature oven, microwave, full-sized sink with hot and cold water, cooled storage, two coffeemakers, and an optional espresso machine. There is even fitted storage space for the dinner service (including crystal and cutlery) custom-made for Gulfstream's private jets.

The Gulfstream 450's Rolls-Royce Tay Mk 611-8C engines are built around the high-pressure engine core of the Spey RB.183-555, which has successfully documented thousands of hours of flight time in various other commercial and private jets. The Rolls-Royce Tay engine, however, gets 2,600 pounds more thrust on takeoff than the Spey. The Tay engines produce 13,850 pounds of thrust each, allowing a sea-level takeoff in 5,450 feet. At an altitude of 5,000 feet, the runway requirement is 8,030 feet. The engines easily meet both FAR part 36 phase III noise requirements, producing 79.1 EPNdB on takeoff, and SFAR part 27 emissions limits. Oil consumption and vibration levels are reportedly low as well.

When the Rolls-Royce Tay Spey RB.183-555 engine is operated during taxi at a 7 percent thrust, a typical twenty-six-minute ground taxi will generate 4.52 g/kg hydrocarbons, 38.97 g/kg of CO_2, and 3.25 g/kg of nitrogen oxides (times two engines). This is also known as the carbon footprint. This will be eliminated when the aircraft is using electrical power for ground taxi operations (see **Appendix Y**).

Gulfstream G500

Also known as the famous GV, the Gulfstream 500 is that last of a long lineage of business jets, starting with the Gulfstream I. Only the fuselage's cross-section remains the same, as the GV is a result of many revisions and redesigns to fill the gap for a larger, intercontinental range executive aircraft. A longer fuselage, modified wing, and new engines are the most noteworthy changes. The GV was certified in 1996 and redesignated the G500 in 2003.

Rolls-Royce engines of the previous Gulfstream models are replaced with the newer BMW/RR BR-700-710-C4-11 turbofan engines. These engines are also used in the Bombardier Global Express, the GV's closest competitor. Each engine is rated at 15,385 pounds of thrust. Inspection intervals are on "on condition" basis.

When the BMW/RR BR-700-710-C4-1 engine is operated during taxi at a 7 percent thrust, a typical twenty six minute ground taxi will generate 4.10 g/kg hydrocarbons, 36.91 g/kg of CO_2, and 3.99 g/kg of nitrogen oxides (times two engines). This is also known as the carbon footprint. This will be eliminated when the aircraft is using electrical power for ground taxi operations (see **Appendix Z**).

Gulfstream 550

Gulfstream is one of the most successful and well-recognized private jet manufacturers and the leader in large-cabin jets. Their aircraft have received exceptional reviews for many years. The Gulfstream G550, an ultra-long-range, intercontinental jet, is the vastly improved iteration of Gulfstream's well-known GV. It can fly faster, farther, more simply, and with more room than its counterpart. Gulfstream created the G550 to combat tough competition in the heavy-iron category in the 1990s. Among its noticeable improvements are enlarged cabin space and more passenger amenities for the ultimate flying experience.

An area that can always be improved/upgraded is the cabin. Cabin space can never be excessive, especially in air travel, and Gulfstream realized this. Significant modifications make the G550 more space-efficient and longer, measuring 42.6 feet. (Height is 6.2 feet and width is 7.3 feet max.) The main entry door was strategically moved two feet forward and the jet employs a new, smaller avionics system, both of which lend fifty-eight more cubic feet of usable cabin space.

Changes in airframe design also yield major improvements, specifically enhancing performance. Topped tanks allow the G550 to travel a greater distance with more passengers than any business jet in production at the time of its release. The G550 can travel 6,750 nautical miles at .80 Mach, with a speed of 460 knots. Its maximum cruise speed is an astounding .87 Mach. The jet is able to complete the 7,301 nm trip from Seoul, South Korea, to Miami, Florida, surpassing the previous record set by its predecessor, the GV. Drag-reducing modifications have also contributed to the G550's exceptional statistics. Engineers reconfigured the cabin pressurization outflow valve so escaping air would provide additional thrust power.

The wing contour has been changed to a more blunt design. Gulfstream fitted the G550 with two BMW/Rolls-Royce BF 700-710-C4-1 turbofan engines. Each is rated at 15,385 pounds of thrust and is inspected "on condition." These engines produce a tremendous amount of power, allowing the jet to travel long-range distances and complete record-breaking missions.

When the BMW/RR BF 700-710-C4-1 engine is operated during taxi at a 7 percent thrust, a typical twenty-six-minute ground taxi will generate 4.10 g/kg hydrocarbons, 36.91 g/kg of CO_2, and 3.99 g/kg of nitrogen oxides (times two engines). This is also known as the carbon footprint. This will be eliminated when the aircraft is using electrical power for ground taxi operations (see **Appendix Z**).

Gulfstream GIV

As the fourth installation in the Gulfstream family line, the GIV offers new advancements that the former aircraft lacked. One of the most significant improvements is the change of engines from the Rolls-Royce Spey to the Rolls-Royce Tay Mk 611-8, used in later jets including the G300 and 400. The successful intercontinental-range business jet has been a prototype for later Gulfstream models.

Two Rolls-Royce Mk 611-8 engines provide 13,850 pounds of thrust each. Inspection interval is 8,000 hours. The Roll-Royce upgraded engine is responsible for 15 percent improved fuel consumption and decreased noise levels (emissions data not available at the time of print)

Gulfstream V

The Gulfstream 500 (or Gulfstream V) was the first contender in the ultra-long-range private jet category. It is capable of flying anywhere in the world: nonstop flights from Denver to Beijing or from New Zealand to San Francisco. It is extremely reliable and high-performing. The ultra-long-range private jet class is a very exclusive and competitive one in which the Gulfstream V competes well.

The 1,669-cubic-foot cabin usually seats fifteen passengers but can be configured to hold more. The stand-up (6.1 feet high) cabin is 50.1 feet long and is usually partitioned into three separate areas. Noise levels are uniformly low throughout the cabin. An external baggage compartment can hold 226 cubic feet of baggage, or a total of 2,500 pounds. Access to this compartment is available in-flight when flying at or above 40,000 feet. Small additional storage compartments are located under each seat.

Two BMW/Rolls-Royce BR710-48 engines, flat-rated to 14,750 pounds of thrust each, provide the power for the Gulfstream V. The engines were designed to be fuel-efficient and reliable. All engine functions are automatically controlled by the dual-channel FADEC.

Runway performance for the Gulfstream V at sea level is 6,110 feet; at an altitude of 5,000 feet, the G-V takes off in 9,150 feet.

It can climb directly to an altitude of 37,000 feet in eighteen minutes, then continue to 43,000 feet for a high-speed cruise of 488 knots or climb to 45,000 feet for a long-range cruise of 459 knots. The highest altitude that it is certified to fly at is 51,000 feet. It is rated to 10.2 psi, meaning that it can maintain a sea-level cabin when flying at 29,200 feet. Cabin pressurization is automatically regulated by a computerized pressurization system.

When the BMW/Rolls-Royce BR710-48 engine is operated during taxi at a 7 percent thrust, a typical twenty-six-minute ground taxi will generate 4.22 g/kg hydrocarbons, 38.91 g/kg of CO_2, and 3.98 g/kg of nitrogen oxides (times two engines). This is also known as the carbon footprint. This will be eliminated when the aircraft is using electrical power for ground taxi operations (see **Appendix AA**).

Dassault Falcon 7X

The 7X employs three Pratt & Whitney Canada PW307A engines. Each engine is rated at 6,402 pounds of thrust. They are responsible for the jet's 5,950 nautical-mile range as well as its fast .90 Mach operating speed. The upgraded engines also reduce cabin noise and vibration, efficient for business travel.

Dassault also improved the Falcon 7X's design, introducing it as the first fully fly-by-wire business jet. The fly-by-wire system gives pilots greater control by limiting the pitch of the aircraft. A completely new wing design and Dassault's first winglets make its long range possible and grant it 35 percent more efficiency than the Falcon 900.

When the Pratt & Whitney Canada PW307A engine is operated during taxi at a 7 percent thrust, a typical twenty-six-minute ground taxi will generate 39.02 g/kg hydrocarbons, 13.01 g/kg of CO_2, 2.61 g/kg of nitrogen oxides, and a smoke number of 1.7.(times three engines). This is also known as the carbon footprint. This will be eliminated when the aircraft is using electrical power for ground taxi operations (see **Appendix BB**).

Airbus A318

The Airbus A318 Elite business jet was launched as a shorter-range, lower-cost option to the successful A319 ACJ. The $45 million A318 is capable of a 4,000 nautical-mile range and .78 Mach cruise speed. The ultra-long-range business jet also boasts a large cabin with room for pull-out sleepers and sofas.

Two CFM International CFM56-5B9 high-bypass engines provide power to the A318. They each produce a forceful 23,300 pounds of thrust and are serviced "on condition." These engines are responsible for the A318's competitive performance stats: .78 Mach cruise speed and 4,000 nm range. The A318 is equipped with avionics manufactured by Northrop Grumman, Thales, and Rockwell Collins. The cockpit is centered around six 7.25-inch LCD displays. Another advantage of the aircraft is its fly-by-wire and steer-by-wire capabilities. Pilots have the option of manual control if a total electrical failure occurs.

When the CFM International CFM56-5B9/3 engine is operated during taxi at a 7 percent thrust, a typical twenty-six-minute ground taxi will generate 3.01 g/kg hydrocarbons, 38.80 g/kg of CO_2, 3.92 g/kg of nitrogen oxides, and a smoke number of 2.1 (times two engines). This is also known as the carbon footprint. This will be eliminated when the aircraft is using electrical power for ground taxi operations (see **Appendix CC**).

Airbus A319

Airbus began as a commercial airliner manufacturer but, after years of experience and success, branched into the corporate ultra-long-range private jet sector with the Airbus A319 Corporate Jetliner (A319CJ). It is a part of the A320 jet family, whose four members have been used collectively by more than twenty airlines, including Frontier Airlines and Air France. The A319CJ is smaller and lighter than the commercial airliner version, giving owners global range capabilities. The A319CJ is a slightly modified version of the A319, an airliner that had more than 130 seats. The corporate version is usually configured to hold eighteen passengers, but exact interior configurations can vary greatly according to an individual's preference.

Since the A319 was originally used by the airlines, much of the interior design in the high-density section of the cabin is reminiscent of commercial airline travel—overhead storage bins, wall partitions, and entertainment screens mounted on the backs of seats. The crossover in design saves a lot of weight and reduces acquisition cost. In addition to the baggage storage inside the jet, such as the overhead bins, there is an external baggage compartment of 160 cubic feet.

When bought new, the A319CJ can be configured with either the International Aero Engines (IAE) V2527M-A5 turbofans or the CFM International CFM56-5B7/P turbofans. The IAEs provide 27,000 pounds of thrust, but are 100 pounds heavier than the CFMI engines. They burn fuel more economically and produce less noise. The CFMI engines produce 26,500 pounds of thrust on takeoff and reportedly need repairs slightly more often than the IAEs but are still well within the margins of airline engine quality and reliability.

When the CFM International CFM56-5B7/P engine is operated during taxi at a 7 percent thrust, a typical twenty-six-minute ground taxi will generate 4.60 g/kg hydrocarbons, 23.40 g/kg of CO_2, 4.30 g/kg of nitrogen oxides, and a smoke number of .5 (times two engines). This is also known as the carbon footprint. This will be eliminated when the aircraft is using electrical power for ground taxi operations (see **Appendix DD**).

Boeing BBJ

The Boeing Business Jet is a member of the venerated 737 family. The 737s collectively have over sixty million hours of flight time and are still in high demand in the commercial aviation market. The BBJ sold more than one hundred planes in just four years of production, and orders continue to come in. No other private jet offers as much cabin space or reliability. After all, the BBJ is a descendant of commercial aircraft, designed to last decades. The Boeing Business Jet's full name is the BBJ 737-700 IGW. IGW stands for "Increased Gross Weight," much of which is due to its massive cabin and increased fuel capacity. The cabin has more square footage than some offices—807 square feet—and measurements well beyond any other private jet: 79.2 feet long, 7.1 feet high, and 11.6 feet wide.

The standard galley, if chosen, comes with a microwave, oven, refrigerator, and freezer, a sink with hot and cold water, food storage, and a trash compactor. Entertainment systems generally include two DVD players, two VCRs, three multidisc CD players, and satellite TV. In other words, the sky is the limit when designing the interior of the BBJ.

The BBJ is powered by two CFM International CFM56-7B27 turbofan engines, each of which provides 27,300 pounds of thrust. CFMI is a partnership between two major jet engine manufacturers: General Electric and SNECMA. They have Flight Authority Digital Engine Control (FADEC), which optimizes their performance and fuel consumption. Any engine-related function which is not controlled by the FADEC, such as thrust adjustments, is automated by the Flight Management System (FMS). This generation of engines has been in use for decades, resulting in no regular required engine maintenance schedules and a 99.9 7 percent dispatch reliability. They are configured to withstand higher temperatures than most of the engines in the CMF56 series and meet FAA noise and emissions standards.

When the CFM International CFM56-7B27 engine is operated during taxi at a 7 percent thrust, a typical twenty-six-minute ground taxi will generate 1.70 g/kg hydrocarbons, 17.90 g/kg of CO_2, 4.80 g/kg of nitrogen oxides, and a smoke number of 0 (times two engines). This is also known as the carbon footprint. This will be eliminated when the aircraft is using electrical power for ground taxi operations (see **Appendix EE**).

Boeing Business Jet 3

The Boeing Business Jet is the product of a Boeing and General Electric joint venture to create a high-performing aircraft. The first BBJ surprised customers and manufacturers by selling more than ever expected.

Introduced in 2006, the ultra-long-range BBJ3 is the largest in the family of Business Jets. It is based on the 737-900ER (Extended Range) airliner.

Capable of traveling large legs, the BBJ3 has a strong powerhouse. It is powered by two General Electric/Snecma (CFMI) CFM56-7B27 engines. Each produces 27,300 pounds of thrust. 5,475 nautical-mile trips, 275nm less than the BBJ2.

When the CFM International CFM56-7B27 engine is operated during taxi at a 7 percent thrust, a typical twenty-six-minute ground taxi will generate 1.70 g/kg hydrocarbons, 17.90 g/kg of CO_2, 4.80 g/kg of nitrogen oxides, and a smoke number of 0 (times two engines). This is also known as the carbon footprint. This will be eliminated when the aircraft is using electrical power for ground taxi operations (see **Appendix EE**).

Embraer Lineage 1000

Embraer, once one of the largest commercial and military aircraft companies in the world, brings thirty-seven years of manufacturing excellence to the aviation industry. In May 2006, Embraer entered the private jet market when they introduced the Lineage 1000, an ultra-large executive jet based on the Embraer 190 regional jet airliner. It surpasses equivalent aircraft in range, cabin size, baggage space, and the ability to indulge. Certified the beginning of 2008, the $43 million Lineage already bodes well with customers.

Apart from its unequaled size, the cabin's amenities epitomize indulgence in travel. There are hundreds of ways to customize the configuration for the ultimate accommodating environment. The cabin is split into five distinctive privacy zones and includes complete audio and entertainment systems, as well as a fully equipped wet galley standard. Plenty of swanky options are available, including three lavatories and a stand-up shower, a queen-size bed, and a high-speed internet connection to accommodate business executives.

Although mentioned above, the 4,200 nautical mile range is worth repeating. Its high-speed cruise is clocked at .82 Mach. The Lineage can take off in 6,660 feet with a maximum takeoff weight (MTOW) of 120,150 pounds. Its high-speed cruise is 470 knots, and it operates at a flight ceiling of 41,000 feet. The Lineage owes credit to its robust engines. Embraer chose General Electric CF34-10E7-B high-bypass jet engines that produce a whopping 18,000 pounds of thrust each. The engines are dual Full Authority Digital Engine Control (FADEC).

When the CFM International General Electric CF34-10E7-B engine is operated during taxi at a 7 percent thrust, a typical twenty-six-minute ground taxi will generate 4.02 g/kg hydrocarbons, 41.73 g/kg of CO_2, 3.69 g/kg of nitrogen oxides, and a smoke number of .5 (times two engines). This is also known as the carbon footprint. This will be eliminated when the aircraft is using electrical power for ground taxi operations (see **Appendix FF**).

CHAPTER 3:

Benefits of the Business Jet Electric Taxi System

The operating costs and environmental initiatives are at the top of the business jet manufacturers and operators' concerns. The business jet electric taxi system provides a viable solution to achieve lower cost and "greener" operations. By adopting this new and innovative aircraft system, aircraft operators can save thousands of dollars per aircraft per year and improve their bottom line, while reducing the environmental impact of airport ground operations. The business jet electric taxi system reduces engine emissions, resulting in a reduction of millions of tons of CO_2, NOx emissions, and lower carbon taxes, while making considerable progress in achieving "carbon-neutral" corporate goals.

Aircraft taxi operations burn a significant amount of fuel—millions of tons of fuel per year. When an aircraft uses the business jet electric taxi system, this can result in savings of up to 4 percent of total fuel consumption. Aircraft equipped with the system will be able to "pushback and go" more quickly, reducing both airport ramp and tarmac congestion, improving on-time departure performance, and saving valuable time on the ground. System operation eliminates the need for aircraft pushback and towing via tug tractor, while also reducing brake wear, extending aircraft usage between maintenance visits, enhancing ground crew safety, and reducing noise in the airport environment. The business jet electric taxi system delivers significant environmental benefits and improves aircraft operating efficiency and increases aircraft usage hours between engine overhauls.

Most of the gasoline- and diesel-powered automobiles made in the past few years will automatically turn off the engine under the hood when the driver stops at a stoplight. Then the engine magically starts up when the driver steps his/her foot on the gas pedal. This saves fuel, reduces exhaust emissions, and preserves the engine operating life. These are some of the same features and benefits of the aircraft electric taxi system when installed and operated on the business jet.

The estimation of fuel consumption and pollutants emitted on the airport's taxiway system is done in four steps: 1. Stopping; 2. Turning; 3. Accelerating; 4. Moving at constant speed or braking.

1. Using detailed surface operations data, calculate the amount of time each aircraft spent on the taxiway. (Stopping, turning, accelerating, moving at constant speed or braking.)
2. Assuming a certain thrust level during each of the four states, extrapolate fuel flow values from International Civil Aviation Organization (ICAO)'s databank.

It is found that stop-and-go situations account for 18 percent of fuel consumed, about 35 percent higher than in situations where aircraft taxi in an unimpeded manner at twenty knots. Idling and taxiing at constant speed or braking are the largest contributors and are sensitive to the thrust level assumptions (ntrs.nasa.gov/api/citations, 2020).

Business Jet Braking System Enhancement

The business jet electric taxi system components can be electronically configured to work as a regenerative braking system, as seen on most modern-day golf carts. A regenerative brake is a mechanism in which the electric motor that drives the vehicle operates in reverse during braking. It is a system of energy recovery that reduces the speed of the vehicle. It is done by transforming the kinetic energy into a form that can be used instantly or stored for later use. The components of regenerative brake systems include an actuator and a storage device. These are required to capture and store energy.

In an electric taxi system, the actuator is the electric machine. The energy storage space is the battery, as it is the aircraft's basic electrical power source. Regenerative braking is the act of turning a motor into a generator. In this way, it slows down the load that it was driving. Regenerative braking puts a little of the energy back into the traction pack and would put the absorbed energy back into the aircraft batteries. It saves the aircraft brakes from being damaged and gives a boost to the aircraft battery every time the aircraft lands and stops. With the installation of the aircraft electric taxi system, the need for the anti-skid braking system can be eliminated. The above regenerative braking system is currently in use on the new Boeing 787 Dreamliner aircraft.

Currently, the medium to larger business jet aircraft employ an anti-skid brake system to aid in safety and mobility while on the ground. However, the necessity of the anti-skid braking system can be evaluated after the first few aircraft are equipped with the aircraft electric taxi system. Aircraft with the electric taxi system should rely less on the anti-skid braking system after the aircraft lands and comes to a full stop. The aircraft functions of taxiing and steering, normally assisted by the anti-skid braking system, can be handled entirely by the electric taxi system. This could be the focus of a continuing study.

The anti-skid braking system has been important in aircraft safety by addressing speed and traction. Speed reduction without the anti-skid braking system installed is nonlinear, time-varying, and uncertain during the braking process after the aircraft lands on the runway. Overrun incidents in past years occurred mostly on wet runways. Therefore, the confirmation of wet runway or dry runway status is crucial, particularly for civil aircraft to optimize the greatest aircraft tire-to-pavement friction and to be certain about the safety of aircraft braking.

Engineers have found that the robustness, adaptability, and anti-interference ability of the runway status can be improved with the use of the anti-skid braking system by using simulation and dynamometer testing. The reliability and safety granted by the anti-skid braking system can largely be assumed by the electric taxi system, as the electric taxi system can handle most features covered by the anti-skid braking system when the electric taxi system is electronically configured with the regenerative braking feature. The electric motors mounted in the aircraft wheels will power the aircraft off the runway and steer it to the airport terminal, all controlled by the pilot with the aircraft main engines shut down.

Fuel Consumption Evaluation During Ground Taxi

These figures were calculated for a typical 10,000-pound thrust, business jet main engine (X 2).

While taxiing twenty minutes per full trip, main engines consume 24.25 lbs/min (eleven kg/min) on the ground, which is 485 lbs (220 kg), seventy-five gallons of fuel per trip. The average price of Jet A in 2022 is $4.85 per gallon. Fuel costs per plane to taxi will be $363.75 per trip.

Emissions Reduction During Ground Taxi

Business jets that are equipped with the electric taxi system will contribute less to local airport area air pollution as the aircraft carbon footprint is reduced. This contribution should not be underestimated, as continued public awareness and growth in air traffic has made the environment a main focus in the future of the business jet aviation industry. It is widely known that sustaining the long-term growth of air transport depends upon environmental improvements for future acceptability.

During aircraft taxi, the release of exhaust gases in the atmosphere on the airport tarmac is the third most important environmental issue related to the business jet industry. These gases can be seen at most major airports as a brown haze hanging about 500 to 1,500 feet above the airport and surrounding areas. The anticipated doubling of business jet fleets in the next twenty years will certainly bring the issue to the forefront. More fuel-efficient aircraft engines that emit fewer pollutants are currently in design by most business jet engine manufacturers and will help offset the increase from growth in air traffic. The contribution of aviation emissions is expected to be increased by a factor of 1.6 to ten, depending on the fuel use scenario.

In theory, aircraft emissions have declined over time when considering the emissions from transporting one passenger one mile. The overall increase is from a system-wide increase in business jet passenger capacity. Current air quality regulations have focused on local emissions generated in airport vicinities. Aircraft operating cycles are usually identified by two major parts. The Landing-Take-off (LTO) cycle, which includes anything near the airport that takes place below the altitude of 3,000 feet (914 m) above ground level, includes taxi-out and in, takeoff, climb-out, and approach-landing. With the application of the electric taxi system, air pollution created while taxiing on the ground can be eliminated and fuel consumption reduced.

The amount of taxi time varies according to airports. One example, however, comes from a study of commercial jets at Boston Logan airport that spent 30 percent of the total time taxiing on the tarmac before takeoff. This does not include the taxi time to the terminal after landing. Taxi-out time averages around nineteen minutes at Boston Logan airport, with an average of 247 flights per day. In the United States, aircraft taxi time translates into six million metric tons of carbon dioxide, 45,000 metric tons of carbon monoxide, 8,000 metric tons of nitrogen oxides, and 4,000 metric tons of hydrocarbons emitted into the atmosphere on an annual basis.

The electric taxi system can be considered green technology as it uses batteries or an auxiliary power unit for electrical power instead of the main engine for propulsion during ground taxi operations. The auxiliary power unit must be operated to provide cabin air conditioning and functions more efficiently than main engines while in ground mode. The auxiliary power unit (APU) is not allowed to be operational indoors. The airplane can taxi inside the hangar using only battery power.

This optimal operating condition, together with the environmental, social, and economic sustainability achieved with an electric taxi system, makes a positive contribution to the communities that airports serve. Since transport systems exist to provide opportunities for people to make social and economic connections, and since the public increasingly values environmentally friendly practices, consumers may see electric taxi system installations as a step towards saving the environment.

Employees and consumers look for companies that are environmentally friendly in the way they operate and the products they make. Furthermore, businesses are discovering they can realize day-to-day cost savings when they take steps towards saving the environment. In addition, these efforts improve company employee recruitment and retention and help the local environment. Business jet operators that install the electric taxi system to enable green taxiing are setting a good example for their employees as well as their customers.

Real-time pollution reduction evaluations can be conducted, and advantages determined, once the first few electric taxi system equipped aircraft are in service. As this chapter has noted, aircraft currently move across the airport tarmac using the thrust of the main engines or by tow with an airport tug, burning much more fuel than is necessary. Using the aircraft's electrical system, sustained by the auxiliary power unit to drive electric motors, should be preferable.

This configuration would keep the movement of the airplane independent of a tow vehicle, consuming less fuel and producing a lower volume of emissions. One fact is interesting: when the aircraft has an auxiliary power unit to charge the batteries and power the electric wheel drive motors, the gas turbine-powered auxiliary power can be shut down during ground taxi and rely totally on the aircraft batteries to save fuel and to eliminate all pollution generated by the aircraft. Using only batteries for taxi power will also allow the business jet to taxi inside the airplane hangars where starting the main engines and auxiliary power units are always prohibited.

The United Kingdom has set a target for overall CO_2 reductions of 80 percent by 2050, relative to 1990's CO_2 measurement levels. Aviation contributes only about 6.3 percent of the United Kingdom's carbon emissions. While it may be argued that this impact is low, aviation in the United Kingdom is growing at approximately 8 percent annually, and it's projected that growth will make aviation carbon emissions a primary concern.

Most of the United Kingdom's allowable CO_2 emissions will be derived from aviation by 2050. This suggests that aviation will remain in the spotlight for the foreseeable future, and against this background, every sector of the industry will have to act to minimize CO_2 emissions. The adoption of the electric taxi system by United Kingdom–based aircraft could help reduce ground-based emissions by 4 percent annually.

The benefits will not be for the United Kingdom alone. Another study presented a detailed estimation of fuel consumption and emissions during taxi operations using aircraft position data from actual operations at Dallas/Fort Worth International Airport. The study assessed thrust level during each state, fuel flow, and emission index values from the International Civil Aviation Organization's data bank. Ultimately, the study provided a relative comparison of all the taxi phases and their contribution to the total fuel consumption and emissions during main engine thrust taxi. Stop-and-go situations, resulting primarily from congestion on the airport's taxiway system, account for approximately 18 percent of fuel consumed.

Aircraft gas turbine engines are designed and certified for optimum fuel consumption and predicted emissions performance at cruise speed. During the engine certification process, the emissions at idle data are recorded, but there are no minimum or maximum emissions requirements. The states of idling and taxiing at constant speed or braking were found to be the two largest sources of inefficient fuel burn and emissions.

The business jet gas turbine engines do generally combust fuel efficiently, and their jet exhausts have very low smoke emissions. However, pollutant emissions from aircraft at ground level are increasing with aircraft movements. In addition, a large amount of air pollution around airports is also generated by surface traffic. The main pollutant of concern around airports is nitrogen dioxide (NO_2). NO_2 is formed by nitrogen oxide (NOx) emissions from surface traffic, aircraft, and airport operations. Particulate Matter (PM2.5) is also of concern, since particulate emissions from jet exhausts are almost all in this fine fraction.

Nitrogen oxide (NO_x) in the lower atmosphere contributes to the production of ozone; ozone in the lower atmosphere is a pollutant and contributes to global warming. Nitrogen oxides from high-altitude supersonic aircraft are thought to damage the stratospheric ozone layer, the protective layer that filters out harmful radiation from the sun. The International Civil Aviation Organization (ICAO) sets international standards for smoke and certain gaseous pollutants for newly produced large jet engines; it also restricts the venting of raw fuels. The latest standards came into effect in 2013 and apply to engine types certified after this date.

Reductions in emissions from aircraft engines have generally been lower in recent years than in other sectors, where technologies such as selective catalytic reduction and exhaust gas recirculation have been employed. There are also increasing numbers of larger aircraft movements, which have disproportionately higher emissions than smaller aircraft. Environmental Protection UK believes that no developments or alterations to the UK aviation infrastructure, air operations, or flight scheduling should result in a breach of the EU limit values or UK air quality objectives or worsen current breaches. Emissions considered must include direct emissions from aircraft, air-side service vehicles, and the surface access required for airports.

Aviation is also a significant source of carbon dioxide emissions and presents a major threat to government targets in terms of emissions growth. This is for three reasons. Firstly, aviation is predicted to grow significantly; secondly, emissions at altitude however are thought to have a greater effect on climate change than those at ground level; and, finally, there is no practical alternative to kerosene-fueled jet engines currently on the horizon. As other sectors reduce emissions, aviation is therefore likely to become responsible for a far larger proportion of global climate change emissions. Aviation Pollution, Environmental Protection UK (environmental-protection.org.uk, 2021).

Emissions from low-altitude and ground aviation operations are regulated under certification requirements for engines, the *Clean Air Act* tailpipe emission standards for airport vehicles, and off-road standards for ground equipment. Aircraft engine certification requirements address carbon monoxide, hydrocarbons, nitrous oxide, and smoke emissions. The International Civil Aviation Organization (ICAO) established CO_2 emission standards for new aircraft in a two-tier plan. One standard applies to new aircraft already certified and in production.

A more restrictive efficiency standard applies to designs that are certified after January 1, 2020, for commercial jets, and January 1, 2023, for business jets, with each category of aircraft entering service about four years after certification. The efficiency requirements will apply to all new aircraft deliveries starting January 1, 2028. The standards are based on an aircraft's mass and will require on average a 4 percent reduction in the cruise fuel consumption, compared to the performance of new aircraft delivered in 2015. When the aircraft is equipped with the business jet electric taxi system, there will be a noticeable emissions reduction during ground taxi that will make a contribution to the International Civil Aviation Organization CO_2 emissions reduction plan (www.eesi.org/papers/view/fact-sheet-the-growth-in-greenhouse-gas-emissions).

Every 2204.62 pounds (1000 kg) of jet fuel burned releases the following combustion byproducts:

- CO_2 - 6040.66 lbs (2,740 kg)
- CH_4 - 5.73 lbs (2.6 kg)
- NO_x - 0.59 lb (270 g)

Converting an entire fleet saves millions of tons of CO_2 per year.

Recent Green Aviation movement initiatives are gaining momentum in Europe and the US. Global governments are incredibly supportive of the concept of highly visible environmental benefits, especially in aviation. Government credits/grants to aircraft operators for research projects can bring about fresh avenues for emission control.

Airport Area Air Pollution

Business jets that are equipped with the electric taxi system will not contribute to the local airport area air pollution. A team of Indian environmental scientists published an article that stated:

The continued public awareness and growth in air traffic has made the environment a main focus in the future of the commercial aviation industry in India. It is widely known that to sustain the long-term growth of air transport, the aircraft need environmental improvements for future acceptability. The release of exhaust gasses in the atmosphere during aircraft taxi on the airport tarmac is the third most important environmental issue related to gas turbine engine equipped aircraft. (https://indianexpress.com/article/cities/)

The overall increase is from a systemwide increase in aircraft passenger capacity. Current air quality regulations have focused on local emissions generated in airport vicinities. Aircraft operating cycles are usually identified by two major parts. The Landing-Take-off (LTO) cycle includes anything near the airport that takes place below the altitude of 3,000 feet (914 m) above ground level; this includes taxi-out and in, takeoff, climb-out, and approach-landing. With the application of the business jet electric taxi system, air pollution created while taxiing can be eliminated and fuel consumption reduced.

Some airports have become upscale trendy hotspots for travelers. The transport systems exist to provide opportunities for people to make social and economic connections. Increased mobility needs to be scaled against the social, environmental, and economic costs. Anything new that can be considered environmentally friendly would be considered good for the environment.

An environmental research team in the United Kingdom (UK) described how the current methods of moving aircraft across the airport tarmac are to use the thrust of the main engines or tow them with airport tugs. The aircraft burns much more fuel than is needed to roll an airplane at taxiing speed. The authors promote the use of the aircraft's electrical system, sustained by the auxiliary power unit (APU) to drive electric motors. This configuration would keep the movement of the airplane independent of a tow vehicle, consuming less fuel and producing fewer emissions. One fact is interesting, however; the aircraft has an APU to charge the aircraft batteries. The aircraft batteries power the electric wheel drive motors. The gas-turbine-powered APU should not be operational during ground taxi, to save fuel and to eliminate all pollution generated by the aircraft. The electric taxi system operating on a battery alone will eliminate emissions generated by the taxiing aircraft. The team also stated that the UK has set a target for overall CO_2 reductions of 80 percent by 2050, relative to CO2 measurements of 1990 levels. Today, aviation contributes only about 6.3 percent of the UK's carbon emission. It may be argued that this impact is low, but the projected growth in aviation is of growing concern.

A team of environmental researchers in Texas presented a detailed estimation of fuel consumption and emissions during taxi operations using aircraft position data from actual operations at Dallas/Fort Worth International Airport. The assumptions of the thrust level during each state, fuel flow, and emission index values from International Civil Aviation Organization's data bank were extrapolated.

Their study provides a relative comparison of all the taxi phases and their contribution to the total fuel consumption and emissions during main engine thrust taxi. The analysis reveals that stop-and-go situations, resulting primarily from congestion on airport's taxiway system, account for approximately 18 percent of fuel consumed. The states of idling and taxiing at constant speed or braking were found to be the two largest sources of fuel burn and emissions (Nikoleris, Gupta, and Kistler, 2014).

European Environmental Research Input

A team of academic atmospheric environmental researchers in the United Kingdom (UK) focused in on two of the most popular gas turbine engines used in general aviation and the business jet community. These engines are the General Electric CF34-3A1 turbofan engine and the Honeywell TPE331-6-252B turboprop. The engine power states were from 16 to 100 percent engine thrust. Both nucleation and soot mode particles were observed from the emission exhausts of the CF34-3A1 engine, but only soot particle mode was detected from the TPE331-6-252B engine.

For the CF34-3A1 engine, the contribution of soot mode (S2) to total particulate matter (PM) emissions was dominant at high power, while at decreased engine power states nucleation mode organic PM became important. Particulate matter emissions indices of the TPE331-6-252B engine were found to be larger than those of the CF34-3A1 engine. For both engines, medium power conditions (40–60 percent of thrust) yielded the lowest PM emissions.

For the TPE331-6-252B engine, volatile PM components including organic and sulfate were more than 50 percent in mass at low power, while non-volatile black carbon became dominant at high power conditions such as takeoff. The PM is just one of the components that make up the carbon footprint. While the gas turbine engine manufacturers must publish an emissions report for each engine, as the engine is certified for use on the aircraft, there is no requirement to report emissions measurements below 15 percent power (Atmospheric Environment, 160, 9–18. 2021).

Middle Eastern Environmental Research Input

An environmental researcher in Turkey calculated the fuel consumption and emissions of carbon monoxide (CO), nitrogen oxide (NOx), and hydrocarbons (HC) in the taxi-out period of business aircraft at the International Diyarbakir Airport in 2018 and 2019. He calculated performance by determining the engine operating times in the taxi-out period with the flight data obtained from the airport authority. In the analyses, aircraft series and aircraft engine types were determined. The Engine Exhaust

Emission Databank of the International Civil Aviation Authority (ICAO) was used for the calculation.

He found the total fuel consumption in the taxi-out period in 2018 and 2019 was calculated as 525.64 and 463.69 tons, respectively. In 2018, HC, CO, and NOx emissions caused by fuel consumption were found to be 1,109, 10,668, and 2,339 kg, respectively. In 2019, the total HC, CO, and NOx emissions released to the atmosphere during the taxi-out phase were 966, 9,391, and 2,126 kg, respectively. These are all contributions to the business jet carbon footprint.

This researcher's study explains the importance of determining fuel consumption and pollutant emissions by considering engine operating times in the taxi-out period. The study provides aviation authorities with scientific methods to follow in calculating fuel consumption and emissions from aircraft operations.

This study is original in that it calculates fuel consumption and pollutant emissions by determining real-time engine running times in the taxi-out period. In addition, calculations were made with real engine operating times determined in the taxi-out period using real flight data. Determination of fuel consumption and pollutant emissions were made with the real-time engine running data of aircrafts in the taxi-out period (Aircraft Engineering and Aerospace Technology, 113, 12–20, 2021).

We can use table 1 and table 2, listed below, taken from the International Civil Aviation Organization (ICAO) data bank records for the Pratt & Whitney

PW1500G series and the Honeywell HTF7000 series of gas turbine engines. The ICAO records all the aircraft jet engine qualification data at the time the engine design and operational status is certified. This will serve as an example of the typical medium "Honeywell" and large-scale "Pratt & Whitney" business jet main propulsion engine.

MODE	POWER SETTING ($\%F_{oo}$)	TIME (minutes)	FUEL FLOW (kg/s)	EMISSIONS INDICES (g/kg)			
				HC	CO	NO_x	SMOKE NUMBER
TAKE-OFF	100	0.7	0.790	0.10	0.00	28.10	3.4
CLIMB OUT	85	2.2	0.650	0.10	0.10	21.20	2.8
APPROACH	30	4.0	0.230	0.10	1.60	11.10	2.4
IDLE	7	26.0	0.080	0.10	13.00	6.10	2.5
LTO TOTAL FUEL (kg) or EMISSIONS (g)			299	30	1719	4125	-
NUMBER OF ENGINES				3	3	3	3
NUMBER OF TESTS				3	3	3	3
AVERAGE D_p/F_{oo} (g/kN) or AVERAGE SN (MAX)				0.3	15.1	37.6	3.8
SIGMA (D_p/F_{oo} in g/kN, or SN)							
RANGE (D_p/F_{oo} in g/kN, or SN)				0.2-0.4	14.6-15.5	36.5-38.3	1.7-5.7

PW 1500G Emissions Data - Table 1

Listed at the center of the table is the carbon (CO) emissions output. This is the most lethal of the jet engine emissions, and it is at the highest level during idle or 7 percent thrust. The carbon is the main air pollutant component, making up the dark cloud that can be seen hanging over most busy airports in the afternoons.

If we look at the ICAO website and review all the modern-day gas turbine engine exhaust emissions data sheets, the emissions reports are all very simular and scalable to each other, depending on the size of the engine. Most will show the carbon emissions are about twenty-six times (26X) greater at ground taxi speed than they are at cruise power. Although it is required that the box is filled in with the carbon g/kg PPM output readings during engine qualification at 7 percent power setting, today there are no ICAO gas turbine engine certification standards that have to be met, for power settings less than 30 percent.

Honeywell HTF7000 Emissions Data – **Table 2**

MODE	POWER SETTING (%F∞)	TIME (minutes)	FUEL FLOW (kg/s)	EMISSIONS INDICES (g/kg)			
				HC	CO	NOx	SMOKE NUMBER
TAKE-OFF	100	0.7	0.347	0.05	0.56	17.90	13.6
CLIMB OUT	85	2.2	0.288	0.06	0.63	16.17	10.6
APPROACH	30	4.0	0.104	0.12	6.28	8.81	0.7
IDLE	7	26.0	0.048	1.26	33.24	3.91	1.7
LTO TOTAL FUEL (kg) or EMISSIONS (g)			152	100	2678	1388	–
NUMBER OF ENGINES				3	3	3	3
NUMBER OF TESTS				10	10	10	10
AVERAGE Dp/F∞ (g/kN) or AVERAGE SN (MAX)				3.3	87.5	45.4	13.6
SIGMA (Dp/F∞ in g/kN, or SN)				0.6	3.7	2.3	1.5
RANGE (Dp/F∞ in g/kN, or SN)				2.36-4.34	81.73-92.46	39.54-47.24	9.2-13.6

Increased Aircraft Usage Between Engine Overhauls

All business jets are equipped with an engine hour meter, aka "HOBBS." The hour meter is running and keeping track of the engine operating hours regardless of whether the aircraft is sitting on the ground at idle, taxiing, or flying at max speed. These hours are tracked and logged by the aircraft operator. This is necessary to keep up with the scheduled aircraft maintenance operations, related mostly to the various engine checks and overhauls recommended by the aircraft and engine manufacturers.

When the aircraft is equipped with the business jet electric taxi system, the pilot can taxi from inside the hanger or from the aircraft location on the airport tarmac with the main engine turned off. The aircraft can taxi using electric power all the way to the engine run-up area on the airport grounds. This taxi time on the tarmac from the aircraft parking area to the engine run-up area is normally logged with the aircraft engine hour meter as engine runtime, even though it might be simply idle or at less than 10 percent thrust. These taxi hours using the main engines add up along with the engine flight hours. The ICAO uses twenty-six minutes for the average taxi-out time during engine certification. The actual time spent on the ground with the engines running can be anywhere from ten minutes to over two hours, depending on the airport congestion and/or whether conditions.

When the business jet is equipped with the business jet electric taxi system, there will be little or no engine time recorded on the main engine(s) hour meter during taxi operations, because the engines will be turned off. This gives the aircraft operator the additional aircraft usage time between aircraft maintenance visits. The maintenance visits are tracked and mandated by the aircraft manufacturer and engine hours. The results are an increase in aircraft usage time between engine overhauls.

Airport Ground Safety

The potential for incursion incidents and injuries is great on active airport aprons and runways. The associated safety hazards caused by jet blast, vibration, noise, fumes, and intake suction of jet engines are well recognized. Even at idle power, the blast effects, the ingestion, the vibration, and fumes from all sizes of aircraft engines can be significant. As the business jet engine size and power settings are increased, the potential for personal injury and damage increase as well.

The amount of emissions produced is related to the engine running time and the power settings used. When workplaces, such as cargo sheds and engineering facilities, must be open directly in the business jet aircraft ground operations areas, a specific risk assessment is required to determine how best to operate all facilities safely and without risks to health with respect to noise, fumes, and jet blast.

Getting a turbine-powered business jet to move on the ground obviously takes a lot more muscle than lighter, piston airplanes. Pilots flying jets often have to momentarily use breakaway thrust to get the wheels moving. This thrust is a lot higher than normal taxi thrust and usually sits somewhere between 25–40 percent of total engine power, depending on aircraft type, surface conditions, and weight.

Pilots initially apply breakaway thrust to get the wheels moving, and once rolling they bring the power further back to somewhere between idle and 20 percent of total engine power. Breakaway thrust is one of the things you should be most concerned about if you're taxiing behind a turbine aircraft.

According to the business jet industry data, the exhaust hazard area for breakaway thrust extends to 400 feet behind large aircraft. For takeoff thrust, the hazard area extends up to 1,900 feet behind the aircraft. Ground vehicles and light aircraft simply don't stand a chance.

Depending on the aircraft, turbine engines can produce anywhere from 2,000 to over 100,000 pounds of thrust. Hundreds of vehicles and aircraft have been damaged over the years due to exhaust wake (jet blast), and it's something everyone should be aware of when operating around turbine aircraft. The FAA briefly mentions jet blast in their ground safety literature, but doesn't get into much detail. According to the Boeing company, at full thrust, modern jet engines can produce exhaust wake velocities exceeding 400 mph at the exhaust nozzle. A Category 5 hurricane is rated with sustained winds above 155 mph.

Many airports still experience incidents related to unexpected jet blast effects, notably on the tarmac during taxi operations. Jet blast can blow vehicles, equipment, or other objects and cause severe damages or injury to people. Airport planners often state that fulfilling "by design" jet blast limitations are too restrictive. It considerably increases the required safety margins and requires the installation of expensive jet blast fences or the definition of restrictive operational measures. Planners would sometimes rather rely on experience than on simulation results or demonstrated values.

A review of the values provided for different aircraft types revealed noticeable inconsistencies and major differences between jet blast contours of similar aircraft types. For instance, B737-800 and Airbus 320-200 are almost the same in terms of dimensions, mass, and engines—but their breakaway contours diverge significantly. The declared contours for a B747-400 are twice more demanding as for a heavier A380.

The main reason for these differences is that there are no standards to determine jet blast values. Manufacturers' methods are not comparable and in addition inconsistent between their own aircraft models. Furthermore, specific maneuvers on the tarmac (e.g., turns, engine-out operations) are not considered—only a "one-fit-all" value is generally provided. These facts do not mean that simulations are useless but show that some more expertise is required as well as a closer examination of the local operational conditions: turns, aircraft mix, possible pilots' behaviors, procedures, etc.

In selecting which contour values to be used at an airport, some airport designers use a safety-based approach, together with more accurate values-obtained methods (full-flight simulator trials, measurements, consolidated technical research) and considering specific operational conditions and scenarios. The benefits for airports are a more accurate design and a more efficient space utilization, along with fewer operational restrictions— while maintaining or increasing the safety level.

When the business jet is equipped with the electric taxi system, the above safety hazards that are a result of the main engines running while on the ground will be nonexistent. There will be no jet blast to worry about. There will be no fumes or vibration. The overall result will be an increase in airport ground safety.

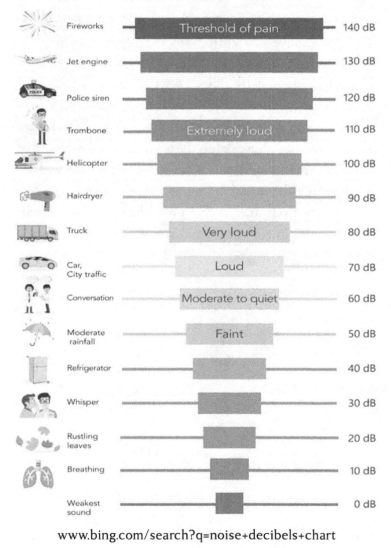

www.bing.com/search?q=noise+decibels+chart

Figure 2

Airport Area Noise Reduction

The primary source of noise on airport aprons is aircraft engines and ground support equipment such as mobile ground power units. The average noise level for a business jet at idle or less than 10 percent thrust, as seen operating at your local airport, is around 130 dB. This could cause a number of impaired hearing issues, depending on how far away you are from the jet engine exhaust outlet. When the business jet is equipped with the electric taxi system, these engine noises at idle will be eliminated.

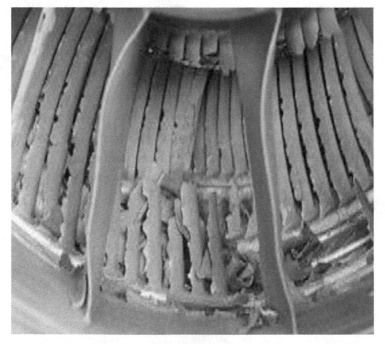

Honeywell HTF7500 Gas Turbine Engine Inlet Guide Vanes
Foreign Object Damage "FOD"
Figure 3

Foreign Object Damage "FOD" Reduction

Foreign object debris, or foreign object damage, both abbreviated to FOD, is a potential source of catastrophic damage to aircraft, particularly to engines. Foreign objects may be ingested into aircraft engines during operation, causing damage leading to engine failure, which is critical if it occurs during the takeoff phase of flight. At best, such damage leads directly to premature engine removal and replacement. The business jet equipped with the electric taxi system will not be incurring any foreign object damage during taxi, because the main engines will be turned off.

Damage caused by foreign object debris at airports can cost the airport tenants and business jet operators millions of dollars every year. When gas turbine engine-equipped aircraft taxi using main engine thrust, the air intake at the front of the engines acts like a giant vacuum cleaner, sucking in air as well as anything on the ground that happens to be in the low-pressure area caused by the turbine intake. Items that are in the range of this negative pressure area are called foreign object debris. According to Bombardier Aircraft Company, foreign object debris can be anything that does not have a purpose in or near an airplane and, as a result, can cause damage to airplanes and injure airline or airport personnel.

Foreign object debris damage can be caused by loose hardware or building materials, sand, rocks, dead animals, and pieces of luggage. Foreign object debris is found at taxiways, cargo aprons, terminal gates, aircraft run-up areas, and runways. Damage caused by foreign object debris is estimated to cost the airline industry over $4 billion a year. Airport tenants and business jet operators can take steps to reduce this cost and prevent this type of damage.

Foreign object damage can also result from objects being caught up in the jet blast and thrown into unpredictable places. The effect of the unplanned damage from foreign object debris can have a catastrophic impact on maintenance costs. For example, to repair an engine damaged by a foreign object could be greater than $1 million. Foreign object debris damage can be a major cause of increased indirect costs through aircraft departure delays and flight cancellations. There is also potential liability, due to additional work and injury for airport staff and management.

Operational Cost Reduction

As of the publish date of this book, no business jet operator or airline is currently operating an aircraft with the electric taxi system installed. Through theory, modeling, and simulation, it has been determined that business jet operators can estimate a 4 percent reduction in total fuel consumption with the electric taxi system installed. Until a business jet is equipped with the electric taxi system and actuals can be evaluated, we can use the 4 percent as a cost reduction baseline.

Gulfstream G650

Figure 4

CHAPTER 4:

Business Jet Aircraft Landing Gear

The business jet landing gear must be strong enough to withstand the forces of landing when the aircraft is fully loaded. In addition to strength, a major design goal is to have the gear assembly be as light as possible. To accomplish this, landing gear are made from a wide range of materials, including steel, aluminum, and magnesium. Wheels and tires are designed specifically for aviation use and have unique operating characteristics.

Main wheel assemblies usually have braking systems. To aid with the potentially high impact of landing, most landing gear have a means of either absorbing shock or accepting shock and distributing it so that the structure is not damaged. The landing gear of most medium to large business jets in current production today have robust enough landing gear assemblies to carry the extra weight of the business jet electric taxi system motors.

As of the print date of this book, there are no aircraft in service utilizing the business jet electric taxi system. During several intense discussions with the business jet original equipment manufacturers (OEMs) and business jet operators, there were pros and cons either for or against the nosewheel drive and the main wheel drive systems.

Nosewheel Drive Installations
Pros

Smaller motors can be used, resulting with smaller electrical inverters. Less weight will be added to the aircraft overall weight. There will be easier installation/integration into the aircraft's existing landing gear systems. The cost will be lower than the main gear installation. The turn radius will be decreased. The nosewheel installation avoids nosewheel damage from tugs.

Cons

The nosewheel-mounted taxi system will achieve a slower taxi speed than the main gear system, and lesser performance in ice, snow, and uphill taxi. There will be slower acceleration. This might be an issue during runway crossing.

Main Gear Drive Installations
Pros

The main-gear-mounted electric taxi system can achieve higher taxi speeds. It allows for higher load capability and better acceleration. There will be improved maneuvering by operating each main gear drive independently. The main gear drive will have improved backup operations.

Cons

The motors and inverters will be larger and more expensive. The main-gear-mounted electric taxi system will require more electric power, add more weight, and generate more heat to the main wheel braking system. The main gear retraction time may be an issue with the aircraft mod and certifications.

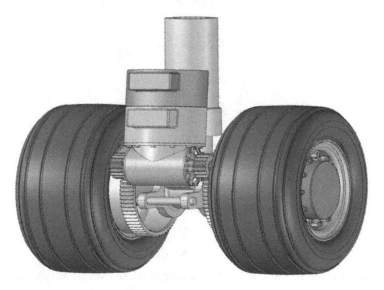

Figure 5
Tandem Gear Drive with Motors Installed

The upper motor is linked with a solid drive shaft. The lower motor is linked with a hollow drive shaft. This will lower the risk of both drive motors becoming nonoperational at the same time.

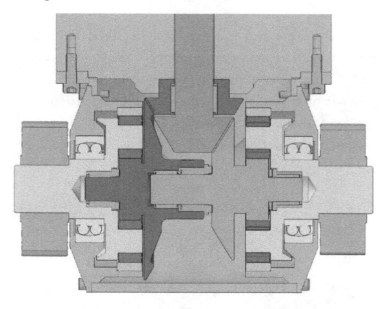

Figure 6
Electric Taxi System Tandem Gear Box Nosewheel

Advantages of the Tandem Gear Box Nosewheel Steering

Lower steering forces are needed to steer the aircraft. The steering operation can be controlled by the actuator, currently incorporated with the standard nosewheel steering. There is built-in fail-safe functionality with two motors. By recording and evaluating exactly the torque of each motor, the lifetime of each component in the system (gears, bearings) could be predicted quite accurately.

Figure 7
Typical Business Jet Main Landing Gear Wheel
with Electric Motors

Figure 8
Embraer Legacy 650

CHAPTER 5:

The Future of the Business Jet Electric Taxi System

Aviation is a significant source of carbon dioxide emissions and presents a major threat to government targets in terms of emissions growth. Aviation is predicted to grow significantly, emissions at altitude are thought to have a greater effect on climate change than those at ground level, and there are no practical alternatives to kerosene-fueled jet engines currently on the horizon. As other sectors reduce emissions, aviation is likely to become responsible for a far larger proportion of global climate change emissions.

The business jet industry has grown tenfold over the past decade. The smaller aircraft jet engine manufacturers have come a long way to increase efficiency and reduce engine weight and fuel consumption, however they are still emitting the same five bad constituents of gas turbine engine (GTE) exhaust emissions, aka carbon footprint.

The electric taxi system kits could be retrofitted for aircraft currently in service or installed at the factory during production. The target-sized aircraft for the aircraft electric taxi system application should be the midsized to large business jets. As of the publish date of this book, no business jet is equipped with the aircraft electric taxi system.

By adopting this new and innovative aircraft system, aircraft operators can save thousands of dollars per aircraft per year and improve their bottom line, while reducing the environmental impact of airport ground operations. The business jet electric taxi system reduces engine emissions, resulting in a reduction of millions of tons of CO_2, NO_x emissions, lower carbon taxes, and making considerable progress in achieving "carbon neutral" corporate goals.

The business jet electric taxi system components can be electronically configured to work as a regenerative braking system, as seen on most modern-day golf carts and the newest Boeing 787. A regenerative brake is a mechanism in which the electric motor that drives the vehicle operates in reverse during braking. The components of regenerative brake systems include an actuator and a storage device. These are required to capture and store energy.

The potential for airport ground incursion incidents and injuries is always a threat on active airport aprons and runways. The associated safety hazards caused by jet blast, vibration, noise, fumes, and intake suction of jet engines are well recognized. Even at idle power, the blast effects, ingestion, vibration, and fumes from all sizes of aircraft engines can be significant. As the business jet engine size and power settings are increased, the potential for personal injury and damage increase as well.

The primary source of noise on airport aprons are aircraft engines and ground support equipment such as mobile ground power units. The average noise level for a business jet at idle or less than 10 percent thrust, as seen operating at your local airport, is around 130 dB. This could cause a number of impaired hearing issues, depending on how far away you are from the jet engine exhaust outlet.

Foreign object debris, or foreign object damage, both abbreviated to FOD, are potential sources of catastrophic damage to aircraft, particularly to engines. Foreign objects may be ingested into aircraft engines during operation, causing damage leading to engine failure, which is critical if it occurs during the takeoff phase of flight. At best, such damage leads directly to premature engine removal and replacement.

As of the print date of this book, there are no aircraft in service utilizing the business jet electric taxi system. During several intense discussions with the business jet original equipment manufacturers (OEMs) and business jet operators, there were pros and cons either for or against the nosewheel drive and the main wheel drive systems. Whether the nosewheel drive or main landing gear wheel drive is selected for system installation, the electric taxi should be a part of the business jet technology evolution to promote "carbon footprint" reduction.

APPENDIX A

ICAO ENGINE EXHAUST EMISSIONS DATA SHEET
Engine Pratt & Whitney Canada JT15D

MODE	POWER SETTING ($\%F_\infty$)	TIME (minutes)	FUEL FLOW (kg/s)	EMISSIONS INDICES (g/kg)			SMOKE NUMBER
				HC	CO	NO_x	
TAKE-OFF	100	0.7	0.148	0.01	2.65	7.60	15.0
CLIMB OUT	85	2.2	0.124	0.01	3.50	6.77	
APPROACH	30	4.0	0.051	4.43	40.50	3.44	
IDLE	7	26.0	0.023	50.50	132.00	1.75	
LTO TOTAL FUEL (kg) or EMISSIONS (g)			71	1866	5306	263	-
NUMBER OF TESTS				1	1	1	1
NUMBER OF ENGINES				1	1	1	1
AVERAGE D_p/F_∞ (g/kN) or AVERAGE SN (MAX)				190.7	542.0	26.9	15.0
SIGMA (D_p/F_∞ in g/kN, or SN)							
RANGE (D_p/F_∞ in g/kN, or SN)							

APPENDIX B

ICAO ENGINE EXHAUST EMISSIONS DATA SHEET
Engine Honeywell TFE731-2-2B

MODE	POWER SETTING ($\%F_{oo}$)	TIME (minutes)	FUEL FLOW (kg/s)	EMISSIONS INDICES (g/kg) HC	CO	NO_x	SMOKE NUMBER
TAKE-OFF	100	0.7	0.205	0.11	1.39	15.25	
CLIMB OUT	85	2.2	0.173	0.13	2.03	13.08	
APPROACH	30	4.0	0.067	4.26	22.38	5.90	
IDLE	7	26.0	0.024	20.04	58.60	2.82	
LTO TOTAL FUEL (kg) or EMISSIONS (g)			85	823	2612	630	–
NUMBER OF ENGINES				3	3	3	
NUMBER OF TESTS				3	3	3	
AVERAGE D_p/F_{oo} (g/kN) or AVERAGE SN (MAX)				53.4	169.4	40.5	
SIGMA (D_p/F_{oo}) in g/kN, or SN							
RANGE (D_p/F_{oo} in g/kN, or SN)				50-58	161-177	39-43	

APPENDIX C

ICAO ENGINE EXHAUST EMISSIONS DATA SHEET
Engine Honeywell TPE 731-3

MODE	POWER SETTING (%F₀₀)	TIME (minutes)	FUEL FLOW (kg/s)	EMISSIONS INDICES (g/kg) HC	EMISSIONS INDICES (g/kg) CO	EMISSIONS INDICES (g/kg) NOₓ	SMOKE NUMBER
TAKE-OFF	100	0.7	0.225	0.06	1.13	19.15	
CLIMB OUT	85	2.2	0.186	0.07	1.62	16.02	
APPROACH	30	4.0	0.072	1.41	15.56	6.92	
IDLE	7	26.0	0.026	9.04	47.70	3.72	
LTO TOTAL FUEL (kg) or EMISSIONS (g)			92	393	2254	845	-
NUMBER OF ENGINES				4	4	4	
NUMBER OF TESTS				4	4	4	
AVERAGE D_p/F_{oo} (g/kN) or AVERAGE SN (MAX)				24.0	137.7	51.4	
SIGMA (D_p/F_{oo} in g/kN, or SN)							
RANGE (D_p/F_{oo} in g/kN, or SN)				19-25	133-147	47-55	

ICAO Aircraft Engine Emissions Databank | EASA (europa.eu)

APPENDIX D

ICAO ENGINE EXHAUST EMISSIONS DATA SHEET
Engine Honeywell TFE 731-40AR200G

MODE	POWER SETTING ($\%F_{oo}$)	TIME (minutes)	FUEL FLOW (kg/s)	EMISSIONS INDICES (g/kg) HC	CO	NO_x	SMOKE NUMBER
TAKE-OFF	100	0.7	0.225	0.05	1.10	19.00	
CLIMB OUT	85	2.2	0.186	0.06	1.50	16.00	
APPROACH	30	4.0	0.072	1.40	15.06	6.00	
IDLE	7	26.0	0.026	9.00	45.70	3.1	
LTO TOTAL FUEL (kg) or EMISSIONS (g)			92	393	2254	845	–
NUMBER OF ENGINES				4	4	4	
NUMBER OF TESTS				4	4	4	
AVERAGE Σ_{Ep}/F_{oo} (g/kN) or AVERAGE SN (MAX)				24.0	137.7	51.4	
SIGMA (D_p/F_{oo} in g/kN, or SN)							
RANGE (D_p/F_{oo} in g/kN, or SN)				19-25	133-147	47-55	

APPENDIX E

ICAO ENGINE EXHAUST EMISSIONS DATA SHEET
Engine Honeywell TFE 731-5B

MODE	POWER SETTING (%F$_{oo}$)	TIME (minutes)	FUEL FLOW (kg/s)	EMISSIONS INDICES (g/kg) HC	CO	NO$_X$	SMOKE NUMBER
TAKE-OFF	100	0.7	0.225	0.05	1.10	19.00	
CLIMB OUT	85	2.2	0.186	0.06	1.50	16.00	
APPROACH	30	4.0	0.072	1.40	15.06	6.00	
IDLE	7	26.0	0.026	9.11	44.70	3.12	
LTO TOTAL FUEL (kg) or EMISSIONS (g)			92	393	2254	845	—
NUMBER OF ENGINES				4	4	4	4
NUMBER OF TESTS				4	4	4	4
AVERAGE D$_p$/F$_{oo}$ (g/kN) or AVERAGE SN (MAX)				24.0	137.7	51.4	
SIGMA (D$_p$/F$_{oo}$ in g/kN, or SN)							
RANGE (D$_p$/F$_{oo}$ in g/kN, or SN)				19-25	133-147	47-55	

ICAO Aircraft Engine Emissions Databank | EASA (europa.eu)

APPENDIX F

ICAO ENGINE EXHAUST EMISSIONS DATA SHEET
Engine Honeywell TFE 731-5R-1H

MODE	POWER SETTING (%F$_{oo}$)	TIME (minutes)	FUEL FLOW (kg/s)	EMISSIONS INDICES (g/kg)			SMOKE NUMBER
				HC	CO	NO$_x$	
TAKE-OFF	100	0.7	0.225	0.05	1.10	19.00	
CLIMB OUT	85	2.2	0.186	0.06	1.50	16.00	
APPROACH	30	4.0	0.072	1.40	15.06	6.00	
IDLE	7	26.0	0.026	8.89	43.60	2.99	
LTO TOTAL FUEL (kg) or EMISSIONS (g)			92	393	2254	845	-
NUMBER OF ENGINES				4	4	4	
NUMBER OF TESTS				4	4	4	
AVERAGE D$_p$/F$_{oo}$ (g/kN) or AVERAGE SN (MAX)				24.0	137.7	51.4	
SIGMA (D$_p$/F$_{oo}$ in g/kN, or SN)							
RANGE (D$_p$/F$_{oo}$ in g/kN, or SN)				19-25	133-147	47-55	

ICAO Aircraft Engine Emissions Databank | EASA (europa.eu)

APPENDIX G

ICAO ENGINE EXHAUST EMISSIONS DATA SHEET
Engine Honeywell TFE 731-5BR

MODE	POWER SETTING (%F∞)	TIME (minutes)	FUEL FLOW (kg/s)	EMISSIONS INDICES (g/kg)			SMOKE NUMBER
				HC	CO	NO_x	
TAKE-OFF	100	0.7	0.225	0.05	1.10	19.00	
CLIMB OUT	85	2.2	0.186	0.06	1.50	16.00	
APPROACH	30	4.0	0.072	1.40	15.06	6.00	
IDLE	7	26.0	0.026	8.88	43.70	2.96	
LTO TOTAL FUEL (kg) or EMISSIONS (g)			92	393	2254	845	-
NUMBER OF ENGINES				4	4	4	
NUMBER OF TESTS				4	4	4	
AVERAGE D_p/F_∞ (g/kN) or AVERAGE SN (MAX)				24.0	137.7	51.4	
SIGMA (D_p/F_∞ in g/kN, or SN)							
RANGE (D_p/F_∞ in g/kN, or SN)				19-25	133-147	47-55	

ICAO Aircraft Engine Emissions Databank | EASA (europa.eu)

APPENDIX H

ICAO ENGINE EXHAUST EMISSIONS DATA SHEET
Engine Honeywell TFE 731-50R

MODE	POWER SETTING ($\%F_{oo}$)	TIME (minutes)	FUEL FLOW (kg/s)	EMISSIONS INDICES (g/kg) HC	EMISSIONS INDICES (g/kg) CO	EMISSIONS INDICES (g/kg) NO_x	SMOKE NUMBER
TAKE-OFF	100	0.7	0.225	0.05	1.10	19.00	
CLIMB OUT	85	2.2	0.186	0.06	1.50	16.00	
APPROACH	30	4.0	0.072	1.40	15.06	6.00	
IDLE	7	26.0	0.026	8.89	43.60	2.97	
LTO TOTAL FUEL (kg) or EMISSIONS (g)			92	393	2254	845	–
NUMBER OF ENGINES				4	4	4	
NUMBER OF TESTS				4	4	4	
AVERAGE D_p/F_{oo} (g/kN) or AVERAGE SN (MAX)				24.0	137.7	51.4	
SIGMA (D_p/F_{oo} in g/kN, or SN)							
RANGE (D_p/F_{oo} in g/kN, or SN)				19-25	133-147	47-55	

ICAO Aircraft Engine Emissions Databank | EASA (europa.eu)

ICAO ENGINE EXHAUST EMISSIONS DATA SHEET
Engine Honeywell TFE 731-3A-2B

MODE	POWER SETTING ($\%F_{oo}$)	TIME (minutes)	FUEL FLOW (kg/s)	EMISSIONS INDICES (g/kg)			SMOKE NUMBER
				HC	CO	NO_x	
TAKE-OFF	100	0.7	0.225	0.05	1.10	19.00	
CLIMB OUT	85	2.2	0.186	0.06	1.50	16.00	
APPROACH	30	4.0	0.072	1.40	15.06	6.00	
IDLE	7	26.0	0.026	8.80	43.59	2.99	
LTO TOTAL FUEL (kg) or EMISSIONS (g)			92	393	2254	845	-
NUMBER OF ENGINES				4	4	4	
NUMBER OF TESTS				4	4	4	
AVERAGE D_p/F_{oo} (g/kN) or AVERAGE SN (MAX)				24.0	137.7	51.4	
SIGMA (D_p/F_{oo} in g/kN, or SN)							
RANGE (D_p/F_{oo} in g/kN, or SN)				19-25	133-147	47-55	

APPENDIX J

CAO ENGINE EXHAUST EMISSIONS DATA SHEET
Engine Pratt & Whitney PW305A

MODE	POWER SETTING ($\%F_{oo}$)	TIME (minutes)	FUEL FLOW (kg/s)	EMISSIONS INDICES (g/kg)			SMOKE NUMBER
				HC	CO	NO_x	
TAKE-OFF	100	0.7	0.148	0.01	2.65	7.60	15.0
CLIMB OUT	85	2.2	0.124	0.01	3.50	6.77	
APPROACH	30	4.0	0.051	4.43	40.50	3.44	
IDLE	7	26.0	0.023	50.10	130.01	1.65	
LTO TOTAL FUEL (kg) or EMISSIONS (g)			71	1866	5306	263	-
NUMBER OF ENGINES				1	1	1	1
NUMBER OF TESTS				1	1	1	1
AVERAGE D_p/F_{oo} (g/kN) or AVERAGE SN (MAX)				190.7	542.0	26.9	15.0
SIGMA (D_p-F_{oo} in g/kN, or SN)							
RANGE (D_p-F_{oo} in g/kN, or SN)							

ICAO Aircraft Engine Emissions Databank | EASA (europa.eu)

ICAO ENGINE EXHAUST EMISSIONS DATA SHEET
Engine Honeywell TFE 731-5AR-1C

MODE	POWER SETTING ($\%F_\infty$)	TIME (minutes)	FUEL FLOW (kg/s)	EMISSIONS INDICES (g/kg) HC	CO	NO_x	SMOKE NUMBER
TAKE-OFF	100	0.7	0.225	0.05	1.10	19.00	
CLIMB OUT	85	2.2	0.186	0.06	1.50	16.00	
APPROACH	30	4.0	0.072	1.40	15.06	6.00	
IDLE	7	26.0	0.026	8.90	44.45	2.98	
LTO TOTAL FUEL (kg) or EMISSIONS (g)			92	393	2254	845	-
NUMBER OF ENGINES				4	4	4	
NUMBER OF TESTS				4	4	4	
AVERAGE D_p/F_∞ (g/kN) or AVERAGE SN (MAX)				24.0	137.7	51.4	
SIGMA (D_p/F_∞ in g/kN, or SN)							
RANGE (D_p/F_∞ in g/kN, or SN)				19-25	133-147	47-55	

APPENDIX L

ICAO ENGINE EXHAUST EMISSIONS DATA SHEET
Engine Honeywell ALF 502L

MODE	POWER SETTING ($\%F_{oo}$)	TIME (minutes)	FUEL FLOW (kg/s)	EMISSIONS INDICES (g/kg) HC	CO	NO$_x$	SMOKE NUMBER
TAKE-OFF	100	0.7	0.372	0.06	0.54	18.29	13.6
CLIMB OUT	85	2.2	0.308	0.06	0.61	16.39	10.6
APPROACH	30	4.0	0.107	0.11	6.29	8.74	0.7
IDLE	7	26.0	0.049	0.94	29.28	3.91	1.2
LTO TOTAL FUEL (kg) or EMISSIONS (g)			158	0.94	29.28		-
NUMBER OF ENGINES				2	2	2	2
NUMBER OF TESTS				6	6	6	6
AVERAGE D_p/F_{oo} (g/kN) or AVERAGE SN (MAX)				2.4	74.0	44.9	13.6
SIGMA (D_p/F_{oo} in g/kN, or SN)				0.6	3.5	2.9	0.9
RANGE (D_p/F_{oo} in g/kN, or SN)				1.82-3.24	70.64-79.66	39.63-47.31	11.4-13.6

APPENDIX M

ICAO ENGINE EXHAUST EMISSIONS DATA SHEET
Engine General Electric CF43-1A

MODE	POWER SETTING ($\%F_{oo}$)	TIME (minutes)	FUEL FLOW (kg/s)	EMISSIONS INDICES (g/kg)			SMOKE NUMBER
				HC	CO	NO_x	
TAKE-OFF	100	0.7	0.870	0.05	0.89	19.68	12.7
CLIMB OUT	85	2.2	0.717	0.09	0.77	16.22	6.9
APPROACH	30	4.0	0.239	0.10	4.02	7.94	0.1
IDLE	7	26.0	0.088	4.10	40.71	3.71	0.5
LTO TOTAL FUEL (kg) or EMISSIONS (g)			326	568	6067	3214	-
NUMBER OF ENGINES				1	1	1	1
NUMBER OF TESTS				3	3	3	3
AVERAGE D_p/F_{oo} (g/kN) or AVERAGE SN (MAX)				6.8	72.5	38.4	12.7
SIGMA (D_p/F_{oo} in g/kN, or SN)				0.7	2.5	0.2	1.5
RANGE (D_p/F_{oo} in g/kN, or SN)				6.3-7.6	70-75	38.2-38.7	11.6-14.4

APPENDIX N

ICAO ENGINE EXHAUST EMISSIONS DATA SHEET
Engine General Electric CF24-3

MODE	POWER SETTING (%F_{oo})	TIME (minutes)	FUEL FLOW (kg/s)	EMISSIONS INDICES (g/kg) HC	EMISSIONS INDICES (g/kg) CO	EMISSIONS INDICES (g/kg) NO_x	SMOKE NUMBER
TAKE-OFF	100	0.7	0.870	0.05	0.89	19.68	12.7
CLIMB OUT	85	2.2	0.717	0.09	0.77	16.22	6.9
APPROACH	30	4.0	0.239	0.10	4.02	7.94	0.1
IDLE	7	26.0	0.088	3.99	38.71	3.88	0.5
LTO TOTAL FUEL (kg) or EMISSIONS (g)			326	568	6067	3214	–
NUMBER OF ENGINES				1	1	1	1
NUMBER OF TESTS				3	3	3	3
AVERAGE D_p/F_{oo} (g/kN) or AVERAGE SN (MAX)				6.8	72.5	38.4	12.7
SIGMA (D_p/F_{oo} in g/kN, or SN)				0.7	2.5	0.2	1.5
RANGE (D_p/F_{oo} in g/kN, or SN)				6.3-7.6	70-75	38.2-38.7	11.6-14.4

ICAO Aircraft Engine Emissions Databank | EASA (europa.eu)

APPENDIX O

ICAO ENGINE EXHAUST EMISSIONS DATA SHEET
Engine General Electric CF34-3A1

MODE	POWER SETTING (%Foo)	TIME (minutes)	FUEL FLOW (kg/s)	EMISSIONS INDICES (g/kg)			SMOKE NUMBER
				HC	CO	NO_x	
TAKE-OFF	100	0.7	0.870	0.05	0.89	19.68	12.7
CLIMB OUT	85	2.2	0.717	0.09	0.77	16.22	6.9
APPROACH	30	4.0	0.239	0.10	4.02	7.94	0.1
IDLE	7	26.0	0.088	4.01	41.79	3.60	0.5
LTO TOTAL FUEL (kg) or EMISSIONS (g)			326	568	6067	3214	-
NUMBER OF TESTS				1	1	1	1
NUMBER OF ENGINES				3	3	3	3
AVERAGE D_p/F_{oo} (g/kN) or AVERAGE SN (MAX)				6.8	72.5	38.4	12.7
SIGMA (D_p/F_{oo} in g/kN, or SN)				0.7	2.5	0.2	1.5
RANGE (D_p/F_{oo} in g/kN, or SN)				6.3-7.6	70-75	38.2-38.7	11.6-14.4

ICAO Aircraft Engine Emissions Databank | EASA (europa.eu)

APPENDIX P

ICAO ENGINE EXHAUST EMISSIONS DATA SHEET
Engine General Electric CF34-3B

MODE	POWER SETTING (%F∞)	TIME (minutes)	FUEL FLOW (kg/s)	EMISSIONS INDICES (g/kg) HC	EMISSIONS INDICES (g/kg) CO	EMISSIONS INDICES (g/kg) NOₓ	SMOKE NUMBER
TAKE-OFF	100	0.7	0.870	0.05	0.89	19.68	12.7
CLIMB OUT	85	2.2	0.717	0.09	0.77	16.22	6.9
APPROACH	30	4.0	0.239	0.10	4.02	7.94	0.1
IDLE	7	26.0	0.088	3.99	41.70	3.65	0.5
LTO TOTAL FUEL (kg) or EMISSIONS (g)			326	568	6067	3214	-
NUMBER OF ENGINES				1	1	1	1
NUMBER OF TESTS				3	3	3	3
AVERAGE Dₚ/F∞ (g/kN) or AVERAGE SN (MAX)				6.8	72.5	38.4	12.7
SIGMA (Dₚ/F∞ in g/kN, or SN)				0.7	2.5	0.2	1.5
RANGE (Dₚ/F∞ in g/kN, or SN)				6.3-7.6	70-75	38.2-38.7	11.6-14.4

ICAO Aircraft Engine Emissions Databank | EASA (europa.eu)

ICAO ENGINE EXHAUST EMISSIONS DATA SHEET
Engine General Electric CFE738

MODE	POWER SETTING (%F_{oo})	TIME (minutes)	FUEL FLOW (kg/s)	EMISSIONS INDICES (g/kg) HC	CO	NO_x	SMOKE NUMBER
TAKE-OFF	100	0.7	0.870	0.05	0.89	19.68	12.7
CLIMB OUT	85	2.2	0.717	0.09	0.77	16.22	6.9
APPROACH	30	4.0	0.239	0.10	4.02	7.94	0.1
IDLE	7	26.0	0.088	3.98	40.70	3.85	0.5
LTO TOTAL FUEL (kg) or EMISSIONS (g)			326	568	6067	3214	-
NUMBER OF TESTS				3	3	3	3
NUMBER OF ENGINES				1	1	1	1
AVERAGE D_p/F_{oo} (g/kN) or AVERAGE SN (MAX)				6.8	72.5	38.4	12.7
SIGMA (D_p/F_{oo} in g/kN, or SN)				0.7	2.5	0.2	1.5
RANGE (D_p/F_{oo} in g/kN, or SN)				6.3-7.6	70-75	38.2-38.7	11.6-14.4

APPENDIX R

ICAO ENGINE EXHAUST EMISSIONS DATA SHEET
Engine Pratt & Whitney PW308C

MODE	POWER SETTING (%F$_{oo}$)	TIME (minutes)	FUEL FLOW (kg/s)	EMISSIONS INDICES (g/kg) HC	EMISSIONS INDICES (g/kg) CO	EMISSIONS INDICES (g/kg) NO$_X$	SMOKE NUMBER
TAKE-OFF	100	0.7	0.148	0.01	2.65	7.60	15.0
CLIMB OUT	85	2.2	0.124	0.01	3.50	6.77	
APPROACH	30	4.0	0.051	4.43	40.50	3.44	
IDLE	7	26.0	0.023	49.02	12.01	1.61	
LTO TOTAL FUEL (kg) or EMISSIONS (g)			71	1866	5306	263	–
NUMBER OF ENGINES				1	1	1	1
NUMBER OF TESTS				1	1	1	1
AVERAGE D$_p$/F$_{oo}$ (g/kN) or AVERAGE SN (MAX)				190.7	542.0	26.9	15.0
SIGMA (D$_p$/F$_{oo}$ in g/kN, or SN)							
RANGE (D$_p$/F$_{oo}$ in g/kN, or SN)							

APPENDIX S

ICAO ENGINE EXHAUST EMISSIONS DATA SHEET
Engine Honeywell TFE731-5BR-1C

MODE	POWER SETTING (%F$_{oo}$)	TIME (minutes)	FUEL FLOW (kg/s)	EMISSIONS INDICES (g/kg) HC	EMISSIONS INDICES (g/kg) CO	EMISSIONS INDICES (g/kg) NOx	SMOKE NUMBER
TAKE-OFF	100	0.7	0.225	0.05	1.10	19.00	
CLIMB OUT	85	2.2	0.186	0.06	1.50	16.00	
APPROACH	30	4.0	0.072	1.40	15.06	6.00	
IDLE	7	26.0	0.026	8.90	44.45	2.98	
LTO TOTAL FUEL (kg) or EMISSIONS (g)			92	393	2254	845	-
NUMBER OF ENGINES				4	4	4	
NUMBER OF TESTS				4	4	4	
AVERAGE D$_p$/F$_{oo}$ (g/kN) or AVERAGE SN (MAX)				24.0	137.7	51.4	
SIGMA (D$_p$/F$_{oo}$ in g/kN, or SN)							
RANGE (D$_p$/F$_{oo}$ in g/kN, or SN)				19-25	133-147	47-55	

ICAO Aircraft Engine Emissions Databank | EASA (europa.eu)

APPENDIX T

ICAO ENGINE EXHAUST EMISSIONS DATA SHEET
Engine Honeywell TFE731-60

MODE	POWER SETTING ($\%F_{oo}$)	TIME (minutes)	FUEL FLOW (kg/s)	EMISSIONS INDICES (g/kg) HC	CO	NO_x	SMOKE NUMBER
TAKE-OFF	100	0.7	0.225	0.05	1.10	19.00	
CLIMB OUT	85	2.2	0.186	0.06	1.50	16.00	
APPROACH	30	4.0	0.072	1.40	15.06	6.00	
IDLE	7	26.0	0.026	8.60	41.10	3.11	
LTO TOTAL FUEL (kg) or EMISSIONS (g)			92	393	2254	845	-
NUMBER OF ENGINES				4	4	4	
NUMBER OF TESTS				4	4	4	
AVERAGE D_p/F_{oo} (g/kN) or AVERAGE SN (MAX)				24.0	137.7	51.4	
SIGMA (D_p/F_{oo} in g/kN, or SN)							
RANGE (D_p/F_{oo} in g/kN, or SN)				19-25	133-147	47-55	

APPENDIX U

ICAO ENGINE EXHAUST EMISSIONS DATA SHEET
Engine Rolls-Royce Spey MK 511-8

MODE	POWER SETTING (%F$_{oo}$)	TIME (minutes)	FUEL FLOW (kg/s)	EMISSIONS INDICES (g/kg) HC	EMISSIONS INDICES (g/kg) CO	EMISSIONS INDICES (g/kg) NO$_X$	SMOKE NUMBER
TAKE-OFF	100	0.7	0.412	0.03	0.77	17.17	0.0
CLIMB OUT	85	2.2	0.343	0.03	0.64	14.91	0.0
APPROACH	30	4.0	0.120	0.03	5.63	7.42	0.0
IDLE	7	26.0	0.048	3.42	39.91	3.99	0.0
LTO TOTAL FUEL (kg) or EMISSIONS (g)			165	264	3018	1501	-
NUMBER OF ENGINES				1	1	1	1
NUMBER OF TESTS				3	3	3	3
AVERAGE D$_p$/F$_{oo}$ (g/kN) or AVERAGE SN (MAX)				7.1	81.2	40.4	0.0
SIGMA (D$_p$/F$_{oo}$ in g/kN, or SN)							
RANGE (D$_p$/F$_{oo}$ in g/kN, or SN)							

ICAO Aircraft Engine Emissions Databank | EASA (europa.eu)

APPENDIX V

ICAO ENGINE EXHAUST EMISSIONS DATA SHEET
Engine Rolls-Royce AE3007A1E

MODE	POWER SETTING (%F$_{oo}$)	TIME (minutes)	FUEL FLOW (kg/s)	EMISSIONS INDICES (g/kg) HC	EMISSIONS INDICES (g/kg) CO	EMISSIONS INDICES (g/kg) NO$_X$	SMOKE NUMBER
TAKE-OFF	100	0.7	0.412	0.03	0.77	17.17	0.0
CLIMB OUT	85	2.2	0.343	0.03	0.64	14.91	0.0
APPROACH	30	4.0	0.120	0.03	5.63	7.42	0.0
IDLE	7	26.0	0.048	3.52	37.97	4.26	0.0
LTO TOTAL FUEL (kg) or EMISSIONS (g)			165	264	3018	1501	–
NUMBER OF ENGINES				1	1	1	1
NUMBER OF TESTS				3	3	3	3
AVERAGE L$_p$/F$_{oo}$ (g/kN) or AVERAGE SN (MAX)				7.1	81.2	40.4	0.0
SIGMA (D$_p$/F$_{oo}$ in g/kN, or SN)							
RANGE (D$_p$/F$_{oo}$ in g/kN, or SN)							

ICAO Aircraft Engine Emissions Databank | EASA (europa.eu)

APPENDIX W

ICAO ENGINE EXHAUST EMISSIONS DATA SHEET
Engine Rolls-Royce BR710-20

MODE	POWER SETTING (%F_{oo})	TIME (minutes)	FUEL FLOW (kg/s)	EMISSIONS INDICES (g/kg) HC	CO	NO_x	SMOKE NUMBER
TAKE-OFF	100	0.7	0.412	0.03	0.77	17.17	0.0
CLIMB OUT	85	2.2	0.343	0.03	0.64	14.91	0.0
APPROACH	30	4.0	0.120	0.03	5.63	7.42	0.0
IDLE	7	26.0	0.048	3.99	39.93	4.21	0.0
LTO TOTAL FUEL (kg) or EMISSIONS (g)			165	264	3018	1501	–
NUMBER OF ENGINES				1	1	1	1
NUMBER OF TESTS				3	3	3	3
AVERAGE D_p/F_{oo} (g/kN) or AVERAGE SN (MAX)				7.1	81.2	40.4	0.0
SIGMA (D_p/F_{oo} in g/kN, or SN)							
RANGE (D_p/F_{oo} in g/kN, or SN)							

ICAO Aircraft Engine Emissions Databank | EASA (europa.eu)

APPENDIX X

ICAO ENGINE EXHAUST EMISSIONS DATA SHEET
Engine Rolls-Royce Tay Mark 611-8C

MODE	POWER SETTING ($\%F_{oo}$)	TIME (minutes)	FUEL FLOW (kg/s)	EMISSIONS INDICES (g/kg) HC	CO	NO_x	SMOKE NUMBER
TAKE-OFF	100	0.7	0.412	0.03	0.77	17.17	0.0
CLIMB OUT	85	2.2	0.343	0.03	0.64	14.91	0.0
APPROACH	30	4.0	0.120	0.03	5.63	7.42	0.0
IDLE	7	26.0	0.048	2.98	35.91	3.93	0.0
LTO TOTAL FUEL (kg) or EMISSIONS (g)			165	264	3018	1501	–
NUMBER OF ENGINES				1	1	1	1
NUMBER OF TESTS				3	3	3	3
AVERAGE D_p/F_{oo} (g/kN) or AVERAGE SN (MAX)				7.1	81.2	40.4	0.0
SIGMA (D_p/F_{oo} in g/kN, or SN)							
RANGE (D_p/F_{oo} in g/kN, or SN)							

APPENDIX Y

ICAO ENGINE EXHAUST EMISSIONS DATA SHEET
Engine Rolls-Royce RB-183-555

MODE	POWER SETTING (%F$_{oo}$)	TIME (minutes)	FUEL FLOW (kg/s)	EMISSIONS INDICES (g/kg) HC	EMISSIONS INDICES (g/kg) CO	EMISSIONS INDICES (g/kg) NO$_x$	SMOKE NUMBER
TAKE-OFF	100	0.7	0.412	0.03	0.77	17.17	0.0
CLIMB OUT	85	2.2	0.343	0.03	0.64	14.91	0.0
APPROACH	30	4.0	0.120	0.03	5.63	7.42	0.0
IDLE	7	26.0	0.048	4.52	38.97	3.25	0.0
LTO TOTAL FUEL (kg) or EMISSIONS (g)			165	264	3018	1501	–
NUMBER OF ENGINES				1	1	1	1
NUMBER OF TESTS				3	3	3	3
AVERAGE D$_p$/F$_{oo}$ (g/kN) or AVERAGE SN (MAX)				7.1	81.2	40.4	0.0
SIGMA (D$_p$/F$_{oo}$ in g/kN, or SN)							
RANGE (D$_p$/F$_{oo}$ in g/kN, or SN)							

ICAO Aircraft Engine Emissions Databank | EASA (europa.eu)

APPENDIX Z

ICAO ENGINE EXHAUST EMISSIONS DATA SHEET
Engine Rolls-Royce BR-700-710-C4-1

MODE	POWER SETTING (%F₀₀)	TIME (minutes)	FUEL FLOW (kg/s)	EMISSIONS INDICES (g/kg) HC	EMISSIONS INDICES (g/kg) CO	EMISSIONS INDICES (g/kg) NOₓ	SMOKE NUMBER
TAKE-OFF	100	0.7	0.412	0.03	0.77	17.17	0.0
CLIMB OUT	85	2.2	0.343	0.03	0.64	14.91	0.0
APPROACH	30	4.0	0.120	0.03	5.63	7.42	0.0
IDLE	7	26.0	0.048	4.10	36.91	3.99	0.0
LTO TOTAL FUEL (kg) or EMISSIONS (g)			165	264	3018	1501	-
NUMBER OF TESTS				3	3	3	3
NUMBER OF ENGINES				1	1	1	1
AVERAGE Dₚ/F₀₀ (g/kN) or AVERAGE SN (MAX)				7.1	81.2	40.4	0.0
SIGMA (Dₚ/F₀₀ in g/kN, or SN)							
RANGE (Dₚ/F₀₀ in g/kN, or SN)							

ICAO Aircraft Engine Emissions Databank | EASA (europa.eu)

APPENDIX AA

ICAO ENGINE EXHAUST EMISSIONS DATA SHEET
Engine BMW/Rolls-Royce BR710-48

MODE	POWER SETTING ($\%F_{oo}$)	TIME (minutes)	FUEL FLOW (kg/s)	EMISSIONS INDICES (g/kg)			SMOKE NUMBER
				HC	CO	NO_x	
TAKE-OFF	100	0.7	0.412	0.03	0.77	17.17	0.0
CLIMB OUT	85	2.2	0.343	0.03	0.64	14.91	0.0
APPROACH	30	4.0	0.120	0.03	5.63	7.42	0.0
IDLE	7	26.0	0.048	4.22	38.91	3.98	0.0
LTO TOTAL FUEL (kg) or EMISSIONS (g)			165	264	3018	1501	-
NUMBER OF ENGINES				1	1	1	1
NUMBER OF TESTS				3	3	3	3
AVERAGE D_p/F_{oo} (g/kN) or AVERAGE SN (MAX)				7.1	81.2	40.4	0.0
SIGMA (D_p/F_{oo} in g/kN, or SN)							
RANGE (D_p/F_{oo} in g/kN, or SN)							

APPENDIX BB

ICAO ENGINE EXHAUST EMISSIONS DATA SHEET
Engine Pratt & Whitney PW307A

MODE	POWER SETTING (%F_{oo})	TIME (minutes)	FUEL FLOW (kg/s)	EMISSIONS INDICES (g/kg) HC	CO	NO_x	SMOKE NUMBER
TAKE-OFF	100	0.7	0.148	0.01	2.65	7.60	15.0
CLIMB OUT	85	2.2	0.124	0.01	3.50	6.77	15.0
APPROACH	30	4.0	0.051	4.43	40.50	3.44	
IDLE	7	26.0	0.023	39.02	13.01	2.61	
LTO TOTAL FUEL (kg) or EMISSIONS (g)			71	1866	5306	263	-
NUMBER OF ENGINES				1	1	1	1
NUMBER OF TESTS				1	1	1	1
AVERAGE D_p/F_{oo} (g/kN) or AVERAGE SN (MAX)				190.7	542.0	26.9	15.0
SIGMA (D_p/F_{oo} in g/kN, or SN)							
RANGE (D_p/F_{oo} in g/kN, or SN)							

APPENDIX CC

ICAO ENGINE EXHAUST EMISSIONS DATA SHEET
Engine CFM International CFM56-5B9/3

MODE	POWER SETTING ($\%F_{oo}$)	TIME (minutes)	FUEL FLOW (kg/s)	EMISSIONS INDICES (g/kg)			SMOKE NUMBER
				HC	CO	NO_x	
TAKE-OFF	100	0.7	0.956	0.02	0.16	17.54	11.2
CLIMB OUT	85	2.2	0.793	0.03	0.17	14.76	8.4
APPROACH	30	4.0	0.278	0.07	4.42	8.26	2.1
IDLE	7	26.0	0.095	3.01	38.80	3.92	2.1
LTO TOTAL FUEL (kg) or EMISSIONS (g)			359	452	6047	3377	-
NUMBER OF ENGINES				3	3	3	3
NUMBER OF TESTS				7	7	7	7
AVERAGE D_p/F_{oo} (g/kN) or AVERAGE SN (MAX)				4.4	58.3	32.6	11.2
SIGMA (D_p/F_{oo} in g/kN, or SN)				0.5	2.8	1.1	2.5
RANGE (D_p/F_{oo} in g/kN, or SN)				3.81-4.74	55.2-60.2	31.6-33.8	8.3-12.9

APPENDIX DD

ICAO ENGINE EXHAUST EMISSIONS DATA SHEET

Engine CFM International CFM56-5B7/P

MODE	POWER SETTING (%F$_{oo}$)	TIME (minutes)	FUEL FLOW (kg/s)	EMISSIONS INDICES (g/kg)			SMOKE NUMBER
				HC	CO	NO$_x$	
TAKE-OFF	100	0.7	1.132	0.20	0.90	28.00	5.4
CLIMB OUT	85	2.2	0.935	0.20	0.90	23.20	4.1
APPROACH	30	4.0	0.312	0.50	2.30	10.00	0.2
IDLE	7	26.0	0.104	4.60	23.40	4.30	0.5
LTO TOTAL FUEL (kg) or EMISSIONS (g)			408	818	4123	5641	–
NUMBER OF ENGINES				1	1	1	1
NUMBER OF TESTS				3	3	3	3
AVERAGE D$_n$/F$_{oo}$ (g/kN) or AVERAGE SN (MAX)				6.8	34.3	47.1	5.4
SIGMA (D$_{p}$, F$_{oo}$ in g/kN, or SN)							
RANGE (D$_{p}$, F$_{oo}$ in g/kN, or SN)							

APPENDIX EE

ICAO ENGINE EXHAUST EMISSIONS DATA SHEET
Engine CFM International CFM56-7B27

MODE	POWER SETTING ($\%F_{oo}$)	TIME (minutes)	FUEL FLOW (kg/s)	EMISSIONS INDICES (g/kg) HC	EMISSIONS INDICES (g/kg) CO	EMISSIONS INDICES (g/kg) NOx	SMOKE NUMBER
TAKE-OFF	100	0.7	1.284	0.10	0.20	30.90	15.7
CLIMB OUT	85	2.2	1.043	0.10	0.50	23.70	12.1
APPROACH	30	4.0	0.349	0.10	1.40	11.00	0.0
IDLE	7	26.0	0.116	1.70	17.90	4.80	0.0
LTO TOTAL FUEL (kg) or EMISSIONS (g)			456	335	3436	6719	-
NUMBER OF ENGINES				1	1	1	1
NUMBER OF TESTS				3	3	3	3
AVERAGE D_p/F_{oo} (g/kN) or AVERAGE SN (MAX)				2.8	28.3	55.3	15.7
SIGMA (D_p/F_{oo} in g/kN, or SN)							
RANGE (D_p/F_{oo} in g/kN, or SN)							

ICAO Aircraft Engine Emissions Databank | EASA (europa.eu)

APPENDIX FF

ICAO ENGINE EXHAUST EMISSIONS DATA SHEET
Engine General Electric CF34-10E7-B

MODE	POWER SETTING (%F$_{oo}$)	TIME (minutes)	FUEL FLOW (kg/s)	EMISSIONS INDICES (g/kg) HC	EMISSIONS INDICES (g/kg) CO	EMISSIONS INDICES (g/kg) NO$_x$	SMOKE NUMBER
TAKE-OFF	100	0.7	0.870	0.05	0.89	19.68	12.7
CLIMB OUT	85	2.2	0.717	0.09	0.77	16.22	6.9
APPROACH	30	4.0	0.239	0.10	4.02	7.94	0.1
IDLE	7	26.0	0.088	4.02	41.73	3.69	0.5
LTO TOTAL FUEL (kg) or EMISSIONS (g)			326	568	6067	3214	-
NUMBER OF ENGINES				1	1	1	1
NUMBER OF TESTS				3	3	3	3
AVERAGE D$_p$/F$_{oo}$ (g/kN) or AVERAGE SN (MAX)				6.8	72.5	38.4	12.7
SIGMA (D$_p$/F$_{oo}$ in g/kN, or SN)				0.7	2.5	0.2	1.5
RANGE (D$_p$/F$_{oo}$ in g/kN, or SN)				6.3-7.6	70-75	38.2-38.7	11.6-14.4

ICAO Aircraft Engine Emissions Databank | EASA (europa.eu)

ACKNOWLEDGMENTS

The Boeing Aircraft Company
Embry-Riddle Aeronautical University
Federal Aviation Administration
Green Taxi Solutions
Honeywell Aerospace
Jet Advisors
Morgan James Publishing
Northcentral University
Pratt & Whitney Canada
Spartan College of Aeronautics and Technology
University of Phoenix

ABOUT THE AUTHOR

Dr. Johnson began the forty-plus years in his aerospace carrier at age nineteen, when he earned his private pilot license at John Wayne Airport (SNA). He then enrolled at Spartan College of Aeronautics in Tulsa, Oklahoma, where he earned his FAA Airframe and Powerplant (A&P) license and began to earn his first bachelor's degree. From Spartan he went to work for Parker Aerospace Irvine, California, in the Air & Space & Fuels Lab. He helped to develop and qualify fuel systems for the F-18, the Canadair Challenger, the F117, the B2 Bomber, and others. Later Tom would be with the Parker/Rockwell/NASA team to develop, evaluate, and qualify various liquid nitrogen (NOx) and liquid oxygen (Lox) fuel valves for the space shuttle. Tom would spend the next ten years working for a small aerospace manufacturing company in Glendale, California, as engineering manager and product line manager, where he designed, developed, and evaluated various engine and airframe hardware for Airbus, Boeing, GE, Pratt & Whitney, Rolls-Royce, and others. Tom's aerospace carrier took him to design, develop, evaluate, qualify, and eventually sell various ATA Chapter 28 Fuels and ATA Chapter 38 Water and Waste system components, valves, and measurement devices to the aircraft OEMs and the airline aftermarket. For the next fifteen years Tom was with Honeywell Engines in Phoenix, Arizona, as lead R&D engineer/scientist. His projects included auxiliary power unit (APU) and gas turbine engine (GTE) engine performance improvements, qualifying sustainable aviation fuels (SAF), weight reduction, and improvements in manufacturability. Tom's family lived in Sun Valley, California, until he was eight years old, when they moved to Huntington Beach, California. He grew up riding waves on his surfboard and working numerous boat and engine projects in the family garage. He raised his family in South Orange County, has two daughters and four grandchildren. Today Tom calls Buckeye (West Phoenix), Arizona, his home.

A free ebook edition
is available with the
purchase of this book.

To claim your free ebook edition:

1. Visit MorganJamesBOGO.com
2. Sign your name CLEARLY in the space
3. Complete the form and submit a photo of the entire copyright page
4. You or your friend can download the ebook to your preferred device

A **FREE** ebook edition is available for you
or a friend with the purchase of this print book.

CLEARLY SIGN YOUR NAME ABOVE

Instructions to claim your free ebook edition:
1. Visit MorganJamesBOGO.com
2. Sign your name CLEARLY in the space above
3. Complete the form and submit a photo of this entire page
4. You or your friend can download the ebook to your preferred device

Print & Digital Together Forever.

Snap a photo

Free ebook

Read anywhere